$C_6H_{12}O_6 + 6O_2$

(neck)
shoulder muscles)
Triceps (back, upper arms)
Pectorals (chest)
The Heart
Biceps (arm muscle with two points of attachment)
Latissimus dorsi (back muscle)
Rectus Abdominus (stomach)

Gluteus maximus (buttocks)
Sartorious (thigh, longest muscle in the body)

Hamstrings (back, thighs)

Quadriceps (front thigh)

Gastroncnemius (two calf muscles)

Achilles Tendon (back, attaches calf to heel)

Skull
Frontal bone
Zygoma (cheek)
Maxilla (upper jaw)

Clavicle (collarbone)

Humerus (upper arm)

Ulna (lesser forearm bone)
Radius (main forearm bone)

Carpals (wrist bones)
Illum, pubis, ischium (pelvic bones)

Femur (thigh bone)

Patella (kneecap)

Tibia (main shinbone)

Fibula (calf bone)

Tarsals (ankle bones)
Metatarsals (foot bones)
Phalanges (toe bones)
Calcaneus (heel)

Sperm Cell

Mitochondria: the fuel that gives the sperm energy
Centrioles: involved with meiotic spindle in dividing cell
Nucleus: carries half the human chromosomes
Acrosome: breaks down the outer membrane of the egg

Egg Cell

Perivitelline space: important in preventing penetration by more than one sperm
Zona pellucida: makes sure the sperm fuses with the egg

A woman is born with every egg she will ever ovulate.

Meiotic spindle: also for correct attachment of chromosomes
Cumulus cells: creates a sticky coating necessary for fertilisation.

positive
...arge) and
...).

Electricity is created when ...ctrons move from ...om to atom.

An electric current always finds the easiest path to the ground.

Mexico City

(total population in millions)

Dinos
When: 6...
Location: C...
Mexico
Size of crater
Size of asteroi...
Size of explosio...
times the bigges...
100,000,000 mega...
Level of destructio...
Earth wiped out

2,000km
(1,243 miles)

'Little Boy' Hiroshima B...
When: 08.15am ... August...
Location: Hiroshima...
Size of crater...
Size of b...

500km
(c2 miles)

EVERYTHING YOU NEED TO KNOW ABOUT EVERYTHING YOU NEED TO KNOW ABOUT

EVERYTHING YOU NEED TO KNOW ABOUT EVERYTHING YOU NEED TO KNOW ABOUT

Your world, and everything around it, in a nutshell

Daniel Tatarsky

Illustrated by Steve Russell

PORTICO

Published in the United Kingdom in 2011 by

Portico Books
10 Southcombe Street
London
W14 0RA

An imprint of Anova Books Company Ltd

ISBN 978-190603-299-9

A CIP catalogue record for this book is available
from the British Library.

10 9 8 7 6 5 4 3 2 1

Printed and bound by Everbest Printing Co., Ltd in China

This book can be ordered direct from the publisher at
www.anovabooks.com

'Everything should be made
as simple as possible,
but not simpler.'

Albert Einstein *(1879-1955)*

Contents_

03.0 The Living Earth_

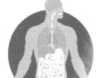

04.0 Humans_

Contents_ *cont.*

Introduction_

How is it possible for the contents of this book to live up to the title?

Let's start by knocking some things on the head. *Everything You Need to Know About Everything You Need to Know About* is not going to help you find your keys [probably in the door], explain why your first girlfriend dumped you [lucky escape for you in all probability], or why everything that is so tasty is also so unhealthy [just live with it]. What this book will attempt to do in just 224 action-packed pages is to give you essential information about this planet, the universe beyond it, and all the things both living and inanimate that make it so unique and wonderfully special.

Research has shown that when people go to art galleries they spend, on average, three times longer reading the art's accompanying caption than looking at the art itself. Further research has shown that we humans retain visual information in our long-term memory quicker than the written word. These two pieces of research seem at first contradictory but when you think about it they actually prove each other.

Our brains can take in a picture, remember it, understand it even, really quickly but the written word needs *processing*. It takes time for us to absorb information and digest it. The written word requires our brain to do a lot more work if we ever want to retrieve the information and put it to use again. In effect, what people usually do is read something, convert it into pictures in their head and then, if it is of interest, try to remember it. So when we look at the *Mona Lisa* we don't need to stare at her indescribable smile for hours to take it in [we only need a few seconds for that] but to retain the details of *who* painted it [come on, you know] when the artist was born and how long it took, takes a little while longer.

It is this dichotomy that we are trying to harness in these pages. Each page, each nugget of information is delivered illustrated, taking advantage of all the exciting ways in which information can now be presented. At a single glance the reader will get to the heart of the facts as well as helping your brain process it quicker, then file the information away, so it is easily retrievable when you next need it for a conversation about, for example, atoms. Accompanying the charts, timelines, diagrams and graphs will be those captions that we all love to read, so that you get the bigger picture too.

This book is for the geek in us all who just wants to know how many people speak Chinese. It's for the big kid that needs to find out what was the biggest dinosaur (and just how big it was!). It's for the history nut who needs to know what date Archduke Ferdinand was assassinated and what were the small increments that then led to a world war.

Everything You Need to Know About Everything You Need to Know About will take you from the Big Bang all the way up to, and just beyond, the Big Crash. It covers a lot of ground and there are a lot of exciting things to discover so we better get started...

Any **bold text** in this book signals the introduction of a key point, person, or concept, which we hope might inspire you to delve further and discover even more than you need to know about everything you need to know about.

Chapter 01.0 Time & Space_

01.1 **Before The Bang_**

Until only very recently the feeling among scientists was that *nothing* existed before the Big Bang – hence the relative emptiness of this page.

However, since **Albert Einstein** published his *Theory of General Relativity* (1915), and with recent advances in scientific debate (most notably Quantum Physics), there are now countless theories about what may have existed *before* the Big Bang. Unfortunately, there is just not enough space here to describe it in effective detail, and indeed what do we *really* know about it after all?

All we can really be sure of is that this tiny black dot – which represents the **entire universe** and contains everything you'll *ever* need to know about – is about to get a whole lot bigger.

[Dot not to scale.]

The Big Bang_

The Big Bang, or When It All Began, took place around 13.7 billion years ago. Because of its name, most people imagine – as we have done here – that the Big Bang was an immense, almighty explosion. However, it wasn't. Instead, it was a **rapid expansion of matter, energy and gases**. The model of the Big Bang Theory is built on the premise that the Universe still appears to be expanding today, and it is from this expansion that scientists have been able to calculate, give or take a few million years, when life in the Universe all began.

Many people forget that the Big Bang is only a theory but, currently, it is by far the most popular and widely supported. The **observable evidence** for how everything began collected so far supports many other theories including, of course, that it was created by one or more gods.

Something To Think About ...

Sir Fred Hoyle is commonly accepted as the person who coined the phrase the 'Big Bang' in 1949. This must have been a source of irritation as he was a strong opponent of the theory. Instead Hoyle was an advocate of the 'Steady State' theory and only came up the 'Big Bang' tag to give a name to the theory he disagreed with.

In The Beginning_

How the Universe was created – according to **the world's six leading religions**.

Almost every religion has, written within its scriptures, a theory of how we all got here.
The unifying element is the presence within these doctrines of a superior being, **the Creator**.
Since science has provided proof of the Big Bang, as well as other explanations of our
existence and evolution, religions – you would think – would have to accept defeat.
But no, faith is still a powerful force.

Be it the Bible, the Qu'ran or the Torah, there are arguments within their pages
that allow the believer to **question the science**. As there is not enough room here
for their entire texts, here are their powerful opening lines:

Christianity ✝
2.4 billion followers

'In the beginning God created the heavens
and the earth. And the earth was without form,
and void … God said, Let there be light!'
Bible, Genesis 1:1

Buddhism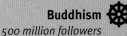
500 million followers

Followers of Buddhism, Buddhists,
believe in the theory of evolution and
have **no theory** regarding
the creation.

Something To Think About …

The Jedi Religion, based on the beliefs of the Jedi Knights in
the *Star Wars* films, now has over 400,000 followers in the UK,
with numbers predicted to rise massively following the next
census in 2011. It was officially recognised as a religion
in 2001.

Sikhism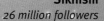
26 million followers

'One Universal Creator God.
The Name Is Truth. Creative Being Personified.
No Fear. No Hatred. Image Of The Undying,
Beyond Birth, Self-Existent.'
Guru Granth Sahib

 Hinduism
900 million followers

'When The Brahman is born, the first
sound he makes is Om, from this all
creation comes.'
Bhagavad-Gita

Judaism ✡
16 million followers

'In the beginning God created the heavens and
the earth. And the earth was without form,
and void ... God said, Let there be light!'
Torah, Genesis 1:1

Islam ☾★
1.15 billion followers

'It is He who created for you all of that which is on
the earth. Then He directed Himself to the heaven,
[His being above all creation], and made them seven
heavens, and He is Knowing of all things.'
Qu'ran, Surat Al-Baqarah 2:2

01.4 The Composition Of Our Universe_

The principle of the **conservation of energy** states that matter can neither be created nor destroyed, it can only be transformed. The essence of this implies that everything that is currently in the Universe has always been here and will always be.

The problem is that since the Big Bang, we now know that the Universe has been **expanding**. This has meant that the amount of **dark matter** as a percentage of the whole has increased, and it is still increasing.

Atoms, e.g. planets, stars, etc., make up just 4.6% of the Universe. Dark Matter accounts for 23% and Dark Energy 72%. Dark Matter is basically stuff we can't see but which has mass. It is not really understood but even less is known about **Dark Energy**. No one really knows what Dark Energy is even though it accounts for nearly three quarters of the Universe. NASA has even set up a mission – the Joint Dark Energy Mission – to try and work it out.

Something To Think About ...

Our knowledge of the Universe is minimal, mainly because we just do not have the capability to travel, or even see far enough to work things out. Research into what is beyond the Universe, or what came before it, is really only carried out by philosophers because it is so far beyond the realms of current scientific reach.

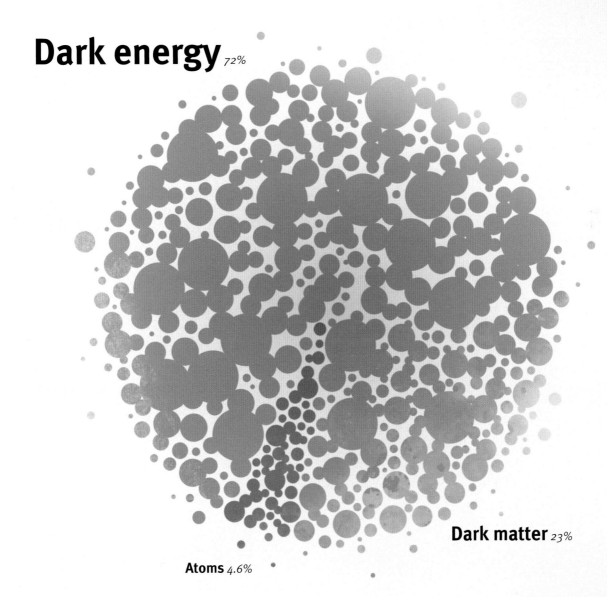

Dark energy *72%*

Dark matter *23%*

Atoms *4.6%*

The Known Galaxies_

A galaxy is a collection of stars, interstellar matter, dust, gas and dark matter, held together as a distinct entity by a **gravitational force**. The number of stars in a galaxy can vary from a few million up to many trillion. Earth is in a solar system that forms part of a galaxy called **the Milky Way**.

In the known Universe there are estimated to be at least a **hundred billion galaxies**, but it is impossible to calculate the exact number.

With advances in telescopes it has been possible to see galaxies many millions of light years away. Some of these galaxies have been named, such as **Hoag's Object**, a ring- shaped galaxy some 600 million light years away.

The Milky Way ....

Something To Think About ...

The Milky Way is about 100,000 light years in diameter. If you laid Milky Way chocolate bars from one end of the galaxy to the other, everyone on Earth would have to eat 6,813 million of them every day (assuming we all lived to be 100) to consume them all.

It's A Fact...

Deep space was opened up to us with the launch of the Hubble Space Telescope in 1990. The telescope orbits Earth every 97 minutes and beams images to several science instruments thanks to its Cassegrain reflector – a unique type of lens configuration.

A telescope works, not by magnifying things, but by collecting more light than the eye can. Hubble's advantage over earthbound scopes is that it is positioned above the Earth's atmosphere, which distorts and filters out much of the light.

The Universe

The Sun_

Earth sits in one of an infinite number of solar systems within the Universe, which we refer to simply as 'The Solar System'. At the centre of all solar systems there is a star, we call ours 'The Sun'.

The Sun is **made up entirely of gas**, most of which is sensitive to magnetism and is called plasma. The two main chemical elements that make up the Sun are **hydrogen** (72% of its mass) and **helium** (26%). The energy of the Sun is created by nuclear fusion within its core. This is when two nuclei combine to form a single nucleus. This fusion converts nuclear matter into energy. The temperature at the surface of the Sun is 5,500°C (9,932°F), at the core it is over 15 million degrees Kelvin.

The Sun contains most of the Solar System's mass (99.8%); it is 330,000 times the mass of Earth, which in terms of relative difference is equivalent to that between a tennis ball and four elephants. In terms of size, the Sun is 109 times bigger than the Earth – imagine a ball on the centre spot of a soccer pitch, with the centre circle representing the Sun. In terms of volume, about 1, 300, 000 Earths would fit inside the Sun.

Something To Think About ...

The Sun's light takes just over eight minutes to reach the Earth. Therefore the light that illuminates your kitchen as you pour your morning cup of coffee actually comes from a point in time before you switched the kettle on.

The Earth

Size: *Diameter 1.4 million km (870,000 miles)*
Composition: *(By Mass) Hydrogen 72%, Helium 26%, Oxygen 1%, Carbon 0.4%*

The Night Sky_

On a clear night the sky is illuminated by a myriad of stars twinkling in far-off space. These stars' relative position to one another appears to remain constant, and so over the years astronomers have grouped them together into constellations, even though in most cases the stars are in fact many light years apart.

By using a system like joining the dots these unconnected stars create objects that can be understood and easily recognised. A familiar sight to most of us, the Plough, or Big Dipper, forms part of the Great Bear constellation, also called Ursa Major. Orion, The Hunter, and his belt is another grouping easily discernable with the naked eye.

Early astronomers believed the Earth was flat with a revolving sky above it. It wasn't until around 570BC that the ancient Greeks calculated that the **Earth was a sphere**. The skies had been studied long before that – initially the Sun and Moon and how their positions related to the seasons. This led to further research into the night sky and eventually **developed into astronomy** as we now know it.

Although the Earth spins on its axis, and travels around the Sun, there are some stars that you are unable to see from the Northern Hemisphere, and some you can't see from the Southern Hemisphere. If you imagine a line that starts from the South Pole and shoots straight out of the North Pole, there is a star, which we call the **North Star**. As the Earth spins, this star appears not to move whilst all the other stars seem to spin around it.

Something To Think About ...

BPM 37093 is the name of a star that seems to have cooled and crystalised thus creating the biggest known diamond. It is around 50 light years from Earth, 4,000km (2,486 miles) in diameter, and has been nicknamed Lucy, named after The Beatles' song 'Lucy in the Sky with Diamonds'.

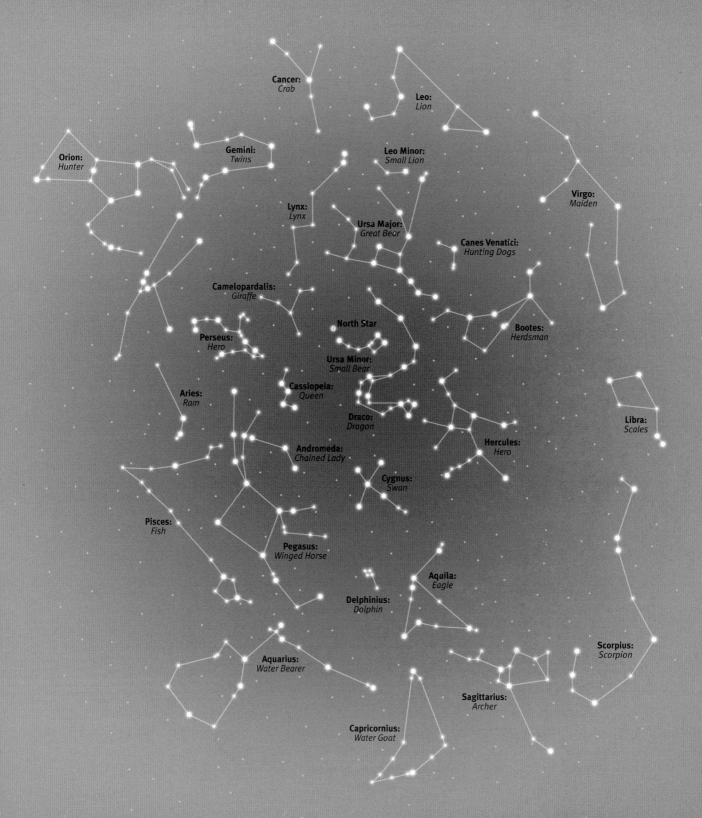

Cancer:
Crab

Leo:
Lion

Orion:
Hunter

Gemini:
Twins

Leo Minor:
Small Lion

Virgo:
Maiden

Lynx:
Lynx

Ursa Major:
Great Bear

Canes Venatici:
Hunting Dogs

Camelopardalis:
Giraffe

North Star

Bootes:
Herdsman

Perseus:
Hero

Ursa Minor:
Small Bear

Aries:
Ram

Cassiopeia:
Queen

Libra:
Scales

Draco:
Dragon

Hercules:
Hero

Andromeda:
Chained Lady

Cygnus:
Swan

Pisces:
Fish

Pegasus:
Winged Horse

Aquila:
Eagle

Delphinius:
Dolphin

Scorpius:
Scorpion

Aquarius:
Water Bearer

Sagittarius:
Archer

Capricornius:
Water Goat

27

The Solar System_

Why is a year on Earth 365 days long? Or more precisely, why is a year on Earth 365.25 days long?

It takes the Earth **365.25 days** to travel one orbit around the Sun. We call this a year. But where does the measurement for a day come from? Well, it takes the Earth 24 hours to make a complete rotation around its axis; let's call it one spin.

Okay, so a day is a spin and a year is an orbit. So how do the planets compare?

The further a planet is away from the Sun the longer its orbit will take and hence the longer its year will last.

To put Pluto's orbit in perspective back here on Earth, if we go back one full orbit for Pluto, on Earth the year would be 1763 and in the UK King George III would be on the throne in England.

What about the length of a day? If you have a bicycle with one little wheel and one big wheel, the small one rotates more quickly, but for the planets the opposite is generally true: **the larger a planet is, the faster it spins**.

Something To Think About ...

Here's a strange one. Venus takes almost 225 days to orbit the Sun but it takes over 243 days to make one spin. What does that mean? In simple terms a day on Venus is longer than a year. Ponder that.

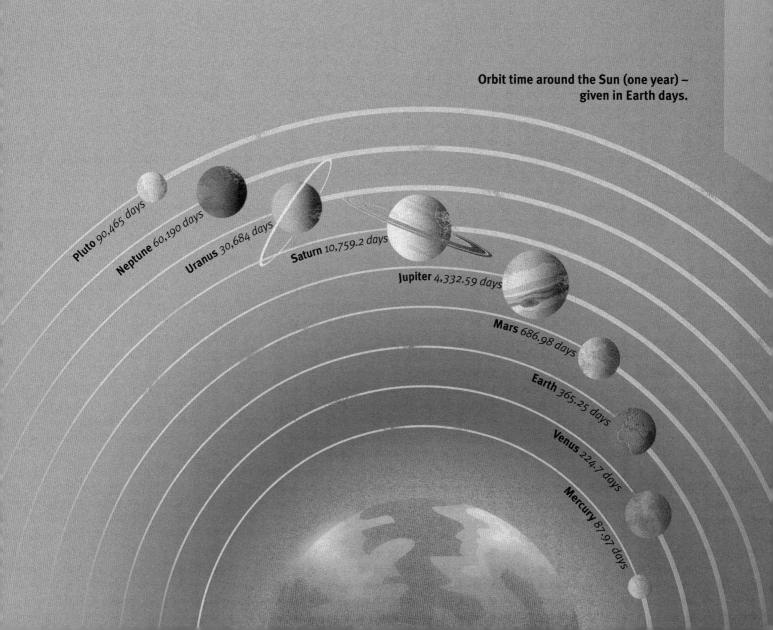

**Orbit time around the Sun (one year) –
given in Earth days.**

Pluto 90,465 days

Neptune 60,190 days

Uranus 30,684 days

Saturn 10,759.2 days

Jupiter 4,332.59 days

Mars 686.98 days

Earth 365.25 days

Venus 224.7 days

Mercury 87.97 days

01.9 Life On Other Planets_

Nobody knows how many planets there are in the Universe but based on the structure of our own Solar System there must be trillions. In our Solar System there are eight planets and one of them definitely has life on it. One in nine suggests good odds of life elsewhere. Even if Earth is the only planet with life on it out of nine million planets, the odds would indicate that there must be life **somewhere else in the Universe**. If this is the case surely we must come across another life form at some point. Not necessarily.

The distances between galaxies, even Solar Systems, and the sheer number of them is such that for two life forms to find each other 'accidentally' would take a near miracle. It would be like one grain of sand on a beach in Miami trying to locate a specific grain on Copacabana beach.

The other thing to note is that we always assume, especially in fiction, that if there are life forms on a distant planet they are more intelligent than humans, and so therefore they will find us. Whilst it is inconceivable that there isn't life somewhere else, there is no reason to suggest that we are not the most advanced. If everything in the Universe comes from the Big Bang, then all the planets that are **capable of supporting life** have had as long as each other to create it. On balance the probability is that there *is* life out there but we will never find it.

Something To Think About ...

In 1961, astrophysicist Frank Drake formulated the Drake Equation. Generally accepted by the scientific community, this equation is a way of mathematically estimating the possible number of technologically advanced beings – sufficient enough to cross the vast void of space – that may exist in our galaxy. The equation looks like this:

$$N = R^* f_p n_e f_l f_i f_c L$$

Dr Drake estimated that there could possibly be 10,000 alien civilisations in our 'local' Milky Way.

The Odds of Alien Life

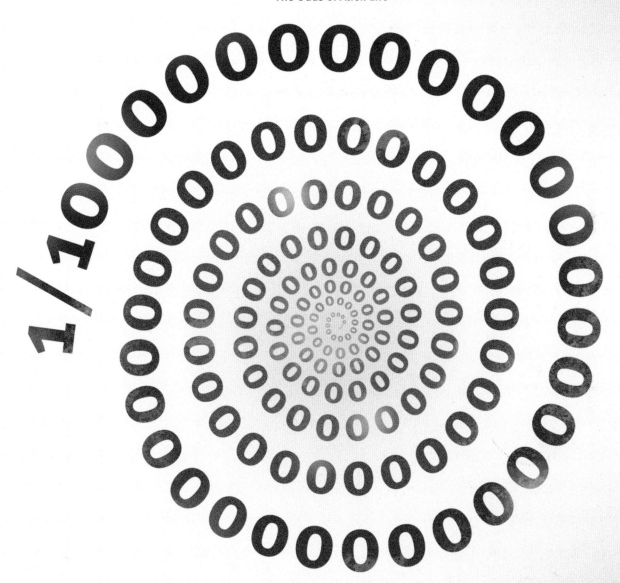

The American astronomer and cosmologist Carl Sagan calculated that
if you were just spontaneously to appear in the Universe, the odds of you being
anywhere near another planet – let alone one with life on – would be
'less than one in a billion trillion trillion' or 10^{33}.

The Planets_

Our Solar System is in the Orion arm of the Milky Way. There are eight planets in our solar system but the count has been as high as 15. This has changed as the definition of a planet has evolved.

At the General Assembly of the **International Astronomical Union** in August 2006 resolution 5a set out a new definition of what a planet is:

(1) *A 'planet' [1] is a celestial body that (a) is in orbit around the Sun, (b) has sufficient mass for its self-gravity to overcome rigid body forces so that it assumes a hydrostatic equilibrium (nearly round) shape, and (c) has cleared the neighbourhood around its orbit.*

Mars

Average Distance from Sun:
228 million km (141,672,632 miles)
Diameter: 6,794km (4,222 miles)
Gravity (compared to Earth): 0.37
Rotation time (in Earth days): 1.0256
Speed: 276.02km/h (171.51mph)

Olympus Mons is the Solar System's largest known volcano.

Venus

Average Distance from Sun:
108 million km (67 million miles)
Diameter: 12,107km (7,523 miles)
Gravity (compared to Earth): 0.88
Rotation time (in Earth days): 243.16
Speed: 2.07km/h (1.29mph)

Days on Venus are longer than years.

Earth

Average Distance from Sun:
150 million km (93,205,679 miles)
Diameter: 12,755km (7,926 miles)
Gravity (compared to Earth): 1
Rotation time (in Earth days): 0.9972
Speed: 531.45km/h (330.26mph)

Mercury

Average Distance from Sun:
58 million km (36 million miles)
Diameter: 4,876km (3,030 miles)
Gravity (compared to Earth): 0.38
Rotation time (in Earth days): 58.6461
Speed: 3.46km/h (2.15mph)

Mainly made of iron, Mercury is the second heaviest planet.

Jupiter

Average Distance from Sun:
778 million km (483,426,788 miles)
Diameter: 142,983km (88,846 miles)
Gravity (compared to Earth): 2.4
Rotation time (in Earth days): 0.4131
Speed: 14,421.75km/h (8,961.26mph)

The Great Red Spot is a storm which has been raging for over 200 years.

As a result of part two of this resolution ...

(2) A 'dwarf planet' is a celestial body that (a) is in orbit around the Sun, (b) has sufficient mass for its self-gravity to overcome rigid body forces so that it assumes a hydrostatic equilibrium (nearly round) shape, (c) has not cleared the neighbourhood around its orbit, and (d) is not a satellite.

Pluto lost its status as a planet and is now classed as a **dwarf planet**.

Neptune

Average Distance from Sun:
4,495 million km (2,793,063,509 miles)
Diameter: 49,527km (30,775 miles)
Gravity (compared to Earth): 1.19
Rotation time (in Earth days): 0.6784
Speed: 3,041.9km/h (1,890.15mph)

Was discovered because of an irregularity in Uranus' orbit which was created by Neptune's gravitational pull.

Saturn

Average Distance from Sun:
1,433 million km (890,424,918 miles)
Diameter: 120,536km (74,898 miles)
Gravity (compared to Earth): 1.07
Rotation time (in Earth days): 0.4257
Speed: 11,797.82km/h (7,330.83mph)

One of Saturn's moons, Titan, is larger than Mercury.

Uranus

Average Distance from Sun: 2,872 million km (1,784,578,064 miles)
Diameter: 51,117km (31,761 miles)
Gravity (compared to Earth): 0.9
Rotation time (in Earth days): 0.7166
Speed: 2,972.2km/h (1,846.84mph)

Unlike all the other planets, Uranus spins on its side in relation to the Sun.

Comets And Collisions_

As it orbits around the Sun once every year, the Earth hurtles through space at 30km (18.5 miles) a second. The distance travelled on this orbital plane is 940 million km (584,088,921 miles). Travelling through so much space, so quickly, it is inevitable that every now and then something will get in our way, or will be on a collision course.

Each year less than 1,000 meteorites hit Earth. Many of these objects burn up as they speed through our atmosphere. However, the larger meteorites that manage to get through and crash land are no bigger than 10m (33ft).

NASA has developed a **monitoring and warning system**, called SENTRY to keep an eye on anything more dangerous that could collide with Earth. SENTRY is an automated system that monitors the paths of Near Earth Objects (NEOs) and plots their course for up to 100 years ahead. If an object appeared that gave rise to a high risk on the **Torino Scale**, right, we would, hopefully, have enough time to react.

Something To Think About ...

The Tunguska Impact is the only observed and verified major impact. It happened on 30 June 1908 in Central Russia, but although it was seen by many people there is no absolute certainty that this was actually a meteorite.

10. Certain collisions
Collision certain, global climatic catastrophe that may threaten the future of civilisation as we know it. Occurs once per 100,000 years.

10

9. Certain collisions
Collision certain, regional devastation for a land impact or the threat of a major tsunami for an ocean impact. Occurs once per 100,000 years.

9

8. Certain collisions
Collision certain, localised destruction for an impact over land or a tsunami if close offshore. Occurs once per several thousand years.

8

7. Threatening
A very close encounter by a large object that poses an unprecedented threat of a global catastrophe.

7

6. Threatening
A close encounter by a large object posing a serious threat of global catastrophe. If less than three decades away, governmental contingency planning warranted.

6

5

5. Threatening
A close encounter posing a serious, but uncertain threat of regional devastation. If less than a decade away, governmental contingency planning warranted.

4

4. Meriting attention by astronomers
A 1% chance of collision capable of regional devastation. Public only notified if less than a decade away.

3

3. Meriting attention by astronomers
A 1% chance of collision capable of localised destruction. A close encounter.

2

2. Meriting attention by astronomers
A discovery of an object making a close pass near the Earth. Actual collision is very unlikely.

1

1. Normal
A routine discovery in which a pass near the Earth is predicted that poses no level of danger or concern.

0

0. No hazard
The likelihood of collision is zero.

The Creation of Planet Earth In Four Easy Steps_

The Bible suggests that the Earth and everything in it, on it, and around it, was created in seven days – or six if you ignore the seventh day when rest was required. Research has indicated that it actually took a little longer.

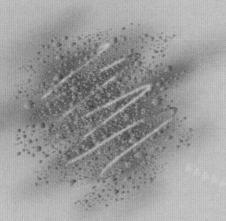

Step 1

Earth, the Sun and the other planets in our Solar System, were formed through the gradual addition of layers due to the force of gravitation from a nebula of gas and dust about 4.6 billion years ago (bya).

Step 2

In the period between 4.5 bya and 1 bya the planet cooled so that now any water that is formed is not instantly evaporated. It is thought that much of our water came from comets – icy masses hurtling through space and crashing into the Earth's surface. During this period photosynthesis was possible.

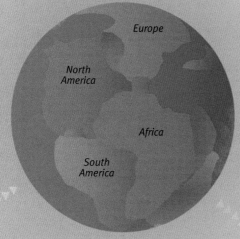

Step 3

About half a bya, life is now evident on the planet in the shape of flora, and the existence of plant life creates more oxygen. It was from around this time onwards that the dinosaurs developed and ruled the Earth. The continents start this period as one, Pangea, but by the end this single continent has broken apart. Sixty-five million years ago, most life on Earth was wiped out when a massive meteorite hit – the dinosaurs' loss was Man's gain.

Step 4

Today. After the dinosaurs died out, and the dust settled, literally, the stage was set for the early development of Man. To get to this point it had taken over four billion years since Earth first came into being – a little more than six days then.

Chapter 02.0 **Our World_**

The Structure And Composition Of Earth_

Every schoolboy and girl knows that the Earth's surface is mainly water. In fact it is just under 71%, with land, therefore, covering 29%. The surface area of the Earth is 510 million sq. km (197 sq. miles) so land covers 149 million sq. km (58 sq. miles).

That tells us about the surface, but what about what is going on underneath? The Earth is made up of five layers, a bit like a golf ball. As we start digging down through the outer layer, the **Crust**, we come to the **Upper Mantle**. The Crust is about 50km (31 miles) thick, it varies from place to place and is thinnest under the oceans. The crust under land comprises **granite**, **basalt** and **diorite** whilst under the oceans it is almost exclusively basalt.

The Upper Mantle is made up of iron and magnesium silicates. It goes down to a depth of 400km (249 miles). Between the Upper Mantle and the Crust is the **Mohorovicic discontinuity** (also known as the Moho) where seismic waves travel at a different and more rapid rate than the Crust or Mantle.

The Lower Mantle comes next and whilst the Upper Mantle is solid, the **Lower Mantle** is fluid. It extends down to a level of almost 3,000km (1,864 miles) and takes us to the **Outer Core**.

The Outer Core is molten lava made up of iron and nickel, and has an average temperature of 5,000°C (9,032°F). It surrounds the **Inner Core**, which is solid iron and nickel, and may reach temperatures as high as the Sun's surface.

Something To Think About ...

Most of the information we have about what goes on beneath our feet is conjecture based on seismological surveys. No one has ever managed to drill through the Crust into the Mantle. As you get deeper the temperature rises, the density of the rock increases and we do not have equipment to cope with this.

Mantle ⋯⋯

The thickest layer of the Earth – made up of moving rock, not lava – is about 1, 800 miles (2, 900km, 1,800 miles) thick. The mantle makes up about 84% of Earth's overall volume. The boundary between the upper mantle and lower mantle lies around 465 miles (750km, 465 miles) below the Earth's surface.

Crust

The crust is the layer of earth away furthest from the hot inner core. Made up of rock, soil and seabed its thickness is about 8km (5 miles) below the ocean and about 50km (31 miles) thick below the continents.

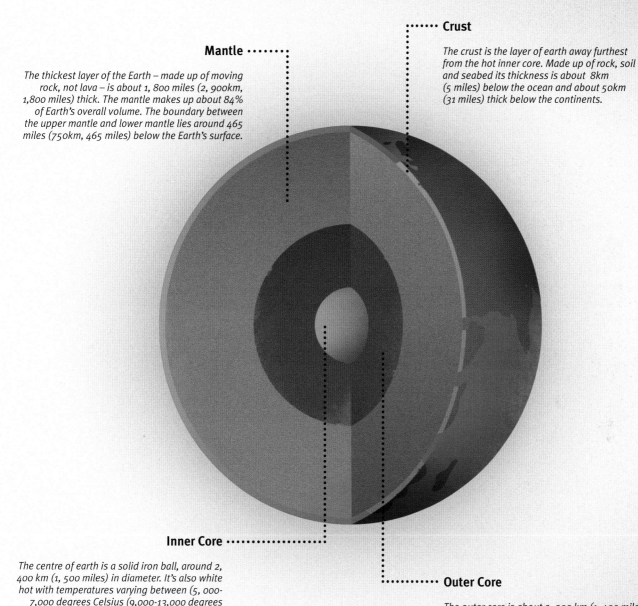

Inner Core ⋯⋯⋯

The centre of earth is a solid iron ball, around 2, 400 km (1, 500 miles) in diameter. It's also white hot with temperatures varying between (5, 000-7,000 degrees Celsius (9,000-13,000 degrees Fahrenheit). Despite the hot temperature the iron is unable to melt due to the massive amounts of pressure that is built up inside.

Outer Core

The outer core is about 2, 300 km (1, 400 miles) thick and surrounds the inner core. It is made up of liquid iron with significant amounts of nickel and sulphur. A lot cooler than the inner core, its temperature is estimated at around 4,000 degrees Celsius (5, 000 degrees Fahrenheit). The outer core creates Earth's vital magnetic field.

02.2 The Atmosphere_

Where does Earth's atmosphere end?

Earth's atmosphere is composed of those gasses that surround the planet and are retained by its gravitational pull. There are **five main layers** that make up the atmosphere and in descending order they are:

Layers of the atmosphere and their approximate altitude

Exosphere ....
Above 500km (311 miles)

Thermosphere ....
85–500km (53–311 miles)
The Karman Line lies in the atmosphere at 100km (62 miles) and defines the boundary between the Earth's atmosphere and outer space.

Mesosphere ....
50–85km (31–53 miles)
The mesosphere rests above the maximum altitude an aircraft can fly.

Stratosphere ....
11–50km (7–31 miles)
Weather balloons go up to around 36km (22 miles).

Troposphere ....
Surface–11km (7 miles)
Commercial airliners fly just below the top.

Something To Think About ...

At an altitude of approximately 19,000m (63,000ft), atmospheric pressure is so low that water boils at the temperature of the human body. This means that exposed body fluids like tears and saliva will begin to boil. This threshold is known as Armstrong's Limit – named after the pioneer of space medicine Harry Armstrong, rather than the astronaut Neil Armstrong.

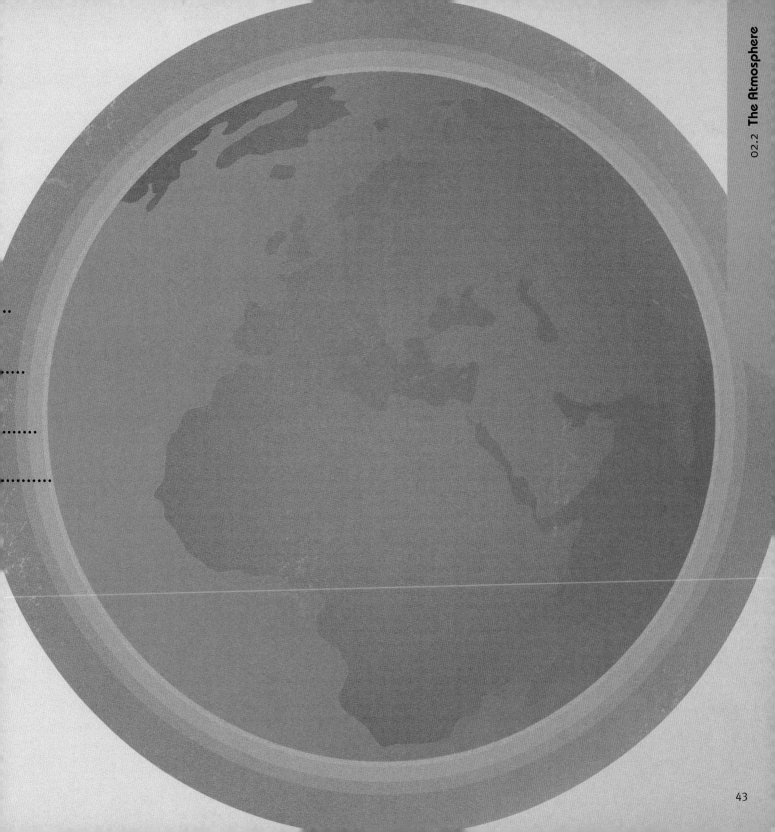

The Continents_

There are now seven continents: **Africa**, the **Americas**, **Antarctica**, **Asia**, **Australia** and **Oceania** (two continents but always discussed as one), and **Europe**. Two hundred and fifty million years ago these continents were a single entity, called **Pangea**.

Continents exist because the Lithosphere, the Upper Crust of the Earth, is split into tectonic plates. These plates 'float' around, which explains the change in the positions of the continents over time. Originally termed 'Continental Drift', the implication was that this movement was quite random. However, as **Plate Tectonics** became the accepted theory, there are now four main ideas about what causes the movement of the continents. These are: convection currents in the Upper Mantle, gravity, the Earth's rotation, and a combination of the three.

North America
Size: *24,700,000 sq. km (9,536,723 sq. miles)*
Population: *530,000,000*
Highest Point: *McKinley (Denali), Alaska (6,194m, 20,320ft)*

South America
Size: *17,800,000 sq. km (6,872,618 sq. miles)*
Population: *390,000,000*
Highest Point: *Aconcagua (6,961m, 22,841ft)*

Something To Think About...

India is on a separate tectonic plate to the rest of Asia. It was the collision of these two plates that created the Himalayas around 55 million years ago, as the Indian plate travelled north and smashed into the Eurasian plate.

Europe
Size: *23,000,000 sq. km (8,880,350 sq. miles)*
Population: *728,000,000*
Highest Point: *Mount El'brus*
(5,624m, 18,510ft)

Asia
Size: *49,700,000 sq. km (19,189,277 sq. miles)*
Population: *4,000,000,000*
Highest Point: *Mount Everest*
(8,848m, 29,029ft)

Africa
Size: *30,200,000 sq. km (11,660,285 sq. miles)*
Population: *885,000,000*
Highest Point: *Mount Kilimanjaro*
(4,602m, 15,100ft)

Australasia
Size: *8,600,000 sq. km (3,320,479 sq. miles)*
Population: *33,000,000*
Highest Point: *Puncak Jaya*
(4,884m, 16,024ft)

Antarctica
Size: *14,000,000 sq. km (5,405,430 sq. miles)*
Population: *0*
Highest Point: *Mount Vinson*
(4,892m, 16,050ft)

45

02.4 The Air We Breathe_

In the simplest terms we are all able to live because we breathe out carbon dioxide, which trees and other plants breathe in. They then breathe out oxygen that we breathe in and so the cycle continues.

The astonishing thing is that the balance of the atmosphere is so stable. It goes to show that the Earth is an incredible **self-regulating mechanism**. While the number of living things on the planet has increased, the amount of oxygen in the air has not gone down, and it is still perfectly balanced to support life on Earth.

Argon *0.934%*

Carbon Dioxide *0.0314%*

Oxygen *20.9476%*

Something To Think About ...

We don't think about breathing, we do it automatically, and we take for granted the supply of clean air. The World Health Organisation estimates that two million deaths a year are attributable to air pollution.

Nitrogen *78.084%*

Other:

Neon *0.001818%*
Methane *0.0002%*
Helium *0.000524%*
Krypton *0.000114%*
Hydrogen *0.00005%*
Xenon *0.0000087%*
Ozone *0.000007%*
Nitrogen Oxide *0.000001%*
Carbon Monoxide *trace*
Ammonia *trace*

The Weather_

The seasons are what makes weather interesting and predictable, although not entirely. Due to a combination of the Earth orbiting the Sun, and the Earth's axis being **slightly tilted**, there are seasons.

These two factors mean that at different times of the year any given place on Earth receives more or less sun each day. This affects temperatures and thus the weather. The variation in temperature between the two extremes becomes less the closer you are to the **Equator**.

There are four seasons, the dates of which vary depending on where on Earth you are. The **Northern and Southern Hemispheres** experience the seasons at opposite times of year.

Summer is when the sun is at its strongest, or rather most proximate for the longest time. Winter is the opposite. Between winter and summer comes spring as the cold retreats and the land begins to warm up. Summer is followed by autumn as the plants and trees that bloom in summer begin to die back. Their petals and leaves die and fall to the ground – hence the American term for the season.

Something To Think About ...

Nephelococcygia is the term applied when people find familiar objects within the shape of a cloud.

Largest snowflake recorded: *38cm x 20cm (15in x 8in)*
28 January 1887 Fort Keogh, Montana, USA

Highest amount of rainfall in 1 min:
31.2mm (1¼ in)
4 July 1956 Unionville, Maryland, USA

Highest amount of rainfall in 1 hour: *305mm (12in)*
22 June 1947 Holt, Missouri, USA

Longest dry period: *173 months*
September 1903–January 1918 Arica, Chile

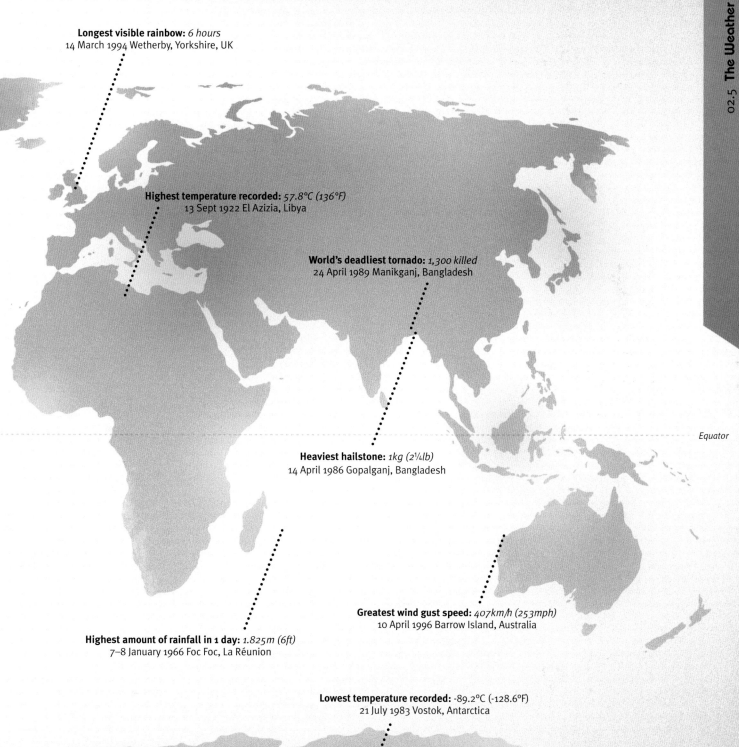

Longest visible rainbow: *6 hours*
14 March 1994 Wetherby, Yorkshire, UK

Highest temperature recorded: *57.8°C (136°F)*
13 Sept 1922 El Azizia, Libya

World's deadliest tornado: *1,300 killed*
24 April 1989 Manikganj, Bangladesh

Equator

Heaviest hailstone: *1kg (2¼lb)*
14 April 1986 Gopalganj, Bangladesh

Greatest wind gust speed: *407km/h (253mph)*
10 April 1996 Barrow Island, Australia

Highest amount of rainfall in 1 day: *1.825m (6ft)*
7–8 January 1966 Foc Foc, La Réunion

Lowest temperature recorded: -89.2°C (-128.6°F)
21 July 1983 Vostok, Antarctica

02.6 The Power Of Earthquakes_

What difference does one point on the Richter Scale make?

Developed in 1935 by **Charles F. Richter** at the California Institute of Technology, the scale compares the magnitude of earthquakes. It goes from one to ten, with one being the weakest magnitude and ten the strongest. An earthquake of Magnitude 10 has never been recorded. The scale is based on logarithms, thus each increase of one on the **magnitude scale** equates to a ten-fold increase in **measured amplitude**.

For those lucky enough never to have been at the site of an earthquake as it happens the following might help compare the forces; it is not meant to equate to them. If Magnitude 1 is a punch in the stomach from a small child, Magnitude 2 is a punch from boxer Mike Tyson at his peak. Keep multiplying it up by ten.

Something To Think About ...

The largest recorded earthquake in the world was in Chile in 1960. The magnitude of the earthquake was measured at 9.5 and created a tsunami so huge that it raced across the Pacific Ocean and devastated Hawaii with waves of up to 11m (35ft).

02.7 Volcanoes_

Deep below the Earth's Crust there lurks hot, liquid rock or **magma**. Like any fluid, magma seeks the route of least resistance and as far as volcanoes are concerned, this is normally at the borders of the tectonic plates. Where magma finds a route out, usually via a random hole in the Earth's Crust known as a **'hot spot'**, a volcano will be formed.

The timescales involved in the formation of a volcano vary wildly, but the best estimates are between 10,000 and 500,000 years, and occur over many hundreds of separate eruptions.

Volcanoes generally fall into one of three categories: **active**, **dormant** or **extinct**. The latter, as the name indicates, covers volcanoes that are regarded as unlikely to erupt again.

Active volcanoes are those that are currently erupting, are exhibiting signs to indicate that an eruption is still likely, or that have erupted in the last 10,000 years. This latter would appear to be a catch all, but because the gap between eruptions can cover a very long period, there is a need to remain cautious.

The difference between an active and a dormant volcano is very uncertain. In effect a dormant volcano is one that may erupt again, but is not currently showing any signs that it might, but which no one is yet convinced it can safely be classed as extinct.

The lifecycle of a volcano generally follows these six stages:

Stage 1
Magma finds a weakness or gap in the Earth's Crust and pushes the rock and earth upwards.

Stage 2
The magma may cool and form a hard crust, which is too heavy for the fluid magma still coming up to burst through, and thus the volcano may die at birth.

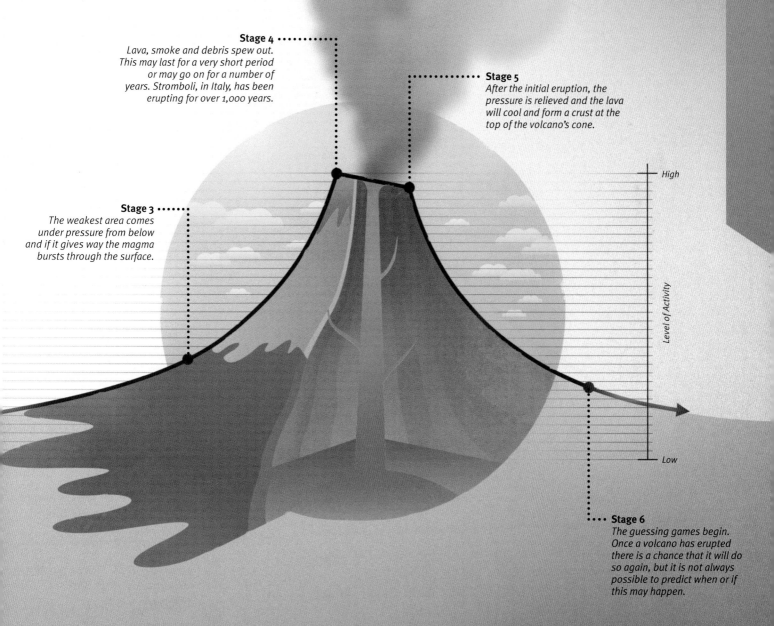

Stage 4
Lava, smoke and debris spew out. This may last for a very short period or may go on for a number of years. Stromboli, in Italy, has been erupting for over 1,000 years.

Stage 5
After the initial eruption, the pressure is relieved and the lava will cool and form a crust at the top of the volcano's cone.

Stage 3
The weakest area comes under pressure from below and if it gives way the magma bursts through the surface.

High

Low

Level of Activity

Stage 6
The guessing games begin. Once a volcano has erupted there is a chance that it will do so again, but it is not always possible to predict when or if this may happen.

An Ocean World_

We all know that the first thing that is vital for life is water. When planet Earth first formed it was dry and there was no water or moisture anywhere. So where did all the water come from?

Over the past 4.6 billion years, there have been many opportunities for water to arrive, or to be produced, on Earth. For many years it was believed that all the water that now forms our oceans was brought by **ice-bearing comets** as the chemical signature of water in the oceans seemed to match that of all known comets.

However, modern-day studies now refute this. The most recent is an analysis of the **comet Hale-Bopp**, which was found to have much more 'heavy hydrogen' than water on Earth, thus making it unlikely that all our water came from comets alone. Some *definitely* did, but not all.

If this is the case then the mystery continues ...

Something To Think About ...

Oceans are salty because the water that fills them up comes from rivers. As this water travels down to the sea it picks up small amounts of salt from the riverbed, which it then carries along with it. Once in the ocean, water is removed by evaporation, but the salt is left behind.

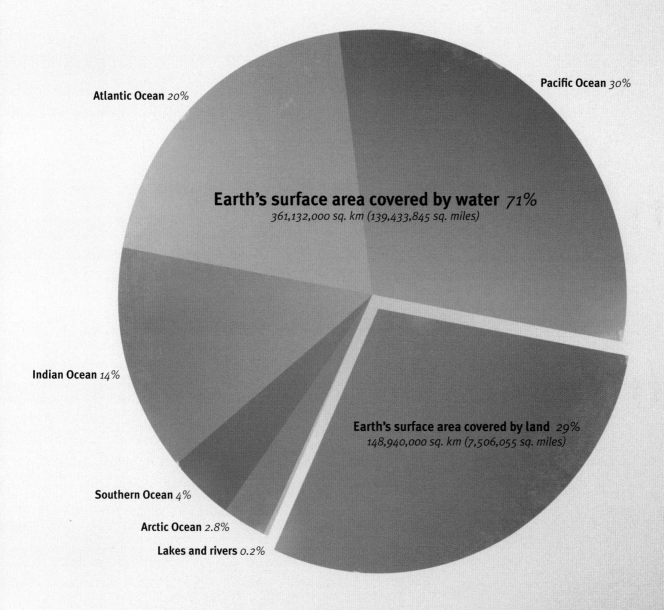

Pacific Ocean *30%*

Atlantic Ocean *20%*

Earth's surface area covered by water *71%*
361,132,000 sq. km (139,433,845 sq. miles)

Indian Ocean *14%*

Earth's surface area covered by land *29%*
148,940,000 sq. km (7,506,055 sq. miles)

Southern Ocean *4%*

Arctic Ocean *2.8%*

Lakes and rivers *0.2%*

The Water Cycle_

The water that exists on the planet today has been here as long, if not a little longer, than there has been life on Earth. The Water Cycle is the planet's **most effective recycling scheme**, and no matter what happens to it, water will always finds its way back into the oceans so the cycle can continue.

So what happens? First, the water in the oceans is heated up by the Sun. This causes **evaporation,** a process whereby the ocean's water changes from a liquid into a gas. The gas rises into the sky and, as the air temperature decreases the higher up you go, the gas cools, **condenses** and returns to a liquid, thereby forming clouds.

As these clouds become bigger and heavier, they reach a point at which they can no longer remain in the air, and the water they contain must fall as **precipitation**. Wherever this falls it will eventually find its way back to rivers, lakes and oceans, and the process begins again.

As well as providing us with drinking water, this cycle is vital for **maintaining the temperature** of the planet. As water evaporates and rises from oceans it takes heat away from the Earth's surface and regulates the atmosphere of the planet much in the same way as sweating keeps the body cool.

Something To Think About ...

The deepest point in the oceans is the Mariana Trench, in the Pacific Ocean, south of Japan. It goes down to a depth of 11km (7 miles). There is room for the whole of Mount Everest with 2km (1.24 miles) to spare.

01. The Sun evaporates ocean water
(evaporation)

02. This moisture rises to create clouds
(condensation)

**05. Water returns to the
ocean via rivers**
(surface runoff and infiltration)

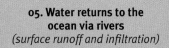

03. Clouds then move inland by wind

**04. Clouds deposit water over
land as rain or snow**
(precipitation)

Lakes And Rivers_

Whilst the vast majority of the world's water exists in the oceans (97%),
our rivers and lakes, although holding only 0.2%* of our water, are still important
to our way of life. For many years rivers provided a **source of energy**, and together with
lakes, have always provided much of our drinking water. They have also been important
for travelling and transporting materials especially in areas where the land does not
offer a viable alternative.

[*The rest is held in glaciers, ice caps and groundwater.]

Lakes form where there is a **natural depression** in the landscape where water collects.

Rivers form when, due to the landscape, the water from lakes, springs and small
tributaries finds a common route down to the sea, another river, or another lake.

World's Longest Rivers

01. **Nile** *6,654km (4,135 miles)* (North/East Africa)

02. **Amazon** *6,405km (3,980 miles)* (South America)

03. **Chang Jiang (Yangtze)** *6,304km (3,917 miles)* (China)

04. **Mississippi-Missouri** *6,228km (3,870 miles)* (USA)

05. **Yenisey** *5,526km (3,434 miles)* (Russia)

06. **Huang He** *5,464km (3,395 miles)* (China)

07. **Ob-Irtysh** *5,398km (3,354 miles)* (Russia)

World's Largest Lakes

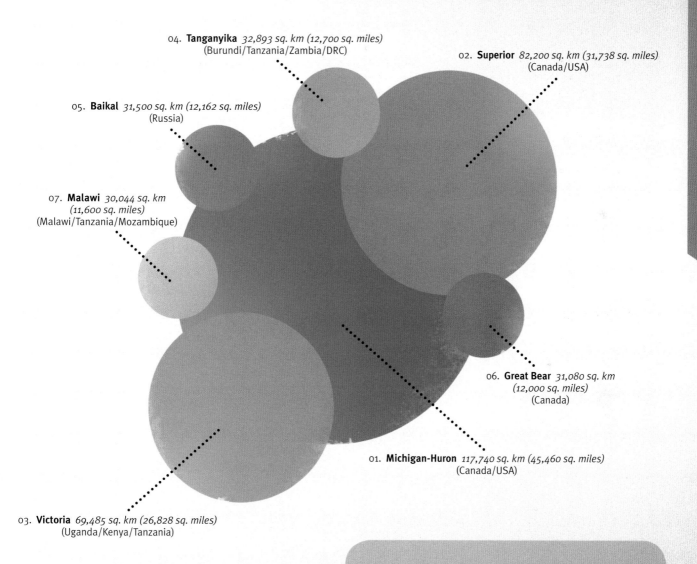

04. **Tanganyika** *32,893 sq. km (12,700 sq. miles)*
(Burundi/Tanzania/Zambia/DRC)

02. **Superior** *82,200 sq. km (31,738 sq. miles)*
(Canada/USA)

05. **Baikal** *31,500 sq. km (12,162 sq. miles)*
(Russia)

07. **Malawi** *30,044 sq. km
(11,600 sq. miles)*
(Malawi/Tanzania/Mozambique)

06. **Great Bear** *31,080 sq. km
(12,000 sq. miles)*
(Canada)

01. **Michigan-Huron** *117,740 sq. km (45,460 sq. miles)*
(Canada/USA)

03. **Victoria** *69,485 sq. km (26,828 sq. miles)*
(Uganda/Kenya/Tanzania)

Something To Think About...

The Roe River, in Great Falls, Montana, USA is the
shortest in the world at a mere 61m (200ft).

The Ice Age Cometh_

We often refer to the Ice Age as though Earth has only ever had one of them. In fact there have been many, and the one we now refer to as 'the' Ice Age is merely the most recent. That ice age is called the **Pleistocene**, and reached its peak around 20,000 years ago, and came to an end about 10,000 years ago.

An ice age is any period where glaciers cover a large part of the Earth and has devastating effects on all living things. As the ice sheet spreads most vegetation is destroyed as it is scraped off the surface by the advancing ice. Because **fauna** depends so much on **flora** for sustenance, animal life is forced to move to warmer areas, but as the ice age extends these diminish. Because so much of the Earth's water becomes frozen, it cannot evaporate and produce rain, which means the planet becomes very dry. Even in these cold, dry, hostile conditions certain creatures can flourish – as the **woolly mammoths** did during the last ice age.

The classic saw-tooth pattern showing the cyclical nature of our planet's weather. This graph illustrates the slow but unstoppable arrival of ice.

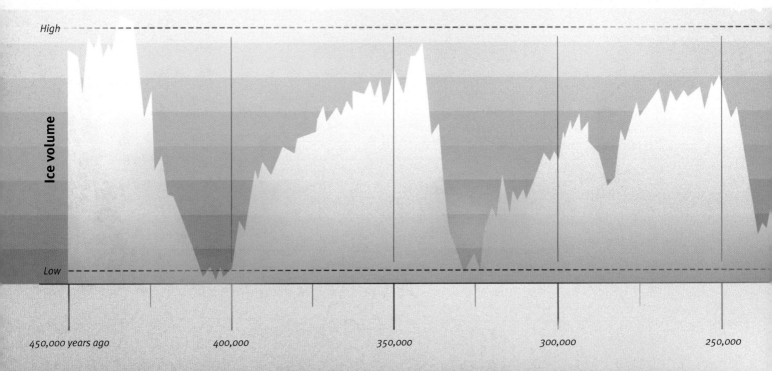

High

Ice volume

Low

450,000 years ago   400,000   350,000   300,000   250,000

The temperature of the planet, and in turn the reappearances of ice ages, is affected by some quirks of Earth's orbit and axis relative to the Sun. These were first reported by Serbian astrophysicist **Milutin Milankovitch**. First there is a 100,000-year cycle caused by variations in the orbit from more to less elliptical and then back again. Secondly there is a 41,000-year cycle due to a quiver or tilt in the orbit of +/-1.5°. Finally, there is a 21,000-year cycle caused by the combination of the first two factors. These combine so that the build-up to an ice age is slow but the end of it is abrupt thus creating a classic, **saw-tooth-shaped graph** seen below.

Something To Think About ...

During the last Ice Age one third of the planet was covered with glaciers. Glaciers currently cover one tenth of the planet, which is why the period we are in now is sometimes referred to as a 'mini ice age'.

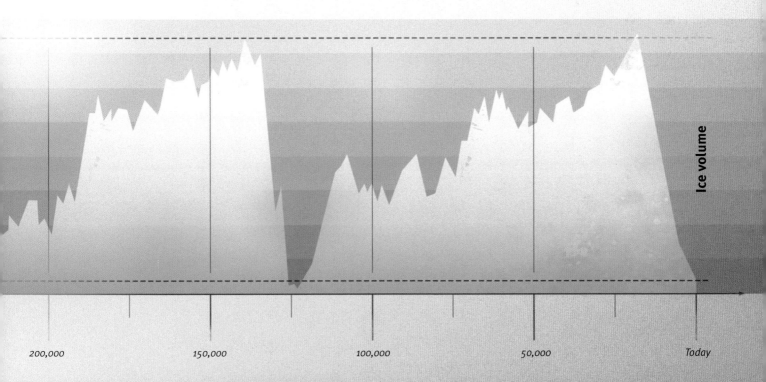

Ice volume

200,000   150,000   100,000   50,000   Today

Seven Natural Wonders Of Our World_

Parícutin

What and Where:
An active, cinder cone volcano in Michoacán, Mexico, 200 miles (321km) west of Mexico City. Has an estimated height of about 3,000 meters (3 km).
Best Time to View:
All year round; rainy season is between May–September.

Parícutin is considered a unique natural wonder of the world as humans witnessed its first eruption in 1943. It has been dormant since 1952.

Aurora Borealis
(also known as the Northern Lights)

What and Where:
Occurring predominantly in the Earth's Ionosphere, the Northern Lights are caused by the colliding of ionized nitrogen atoms with solar-wind particles near Earth's magnetic North and South poles.
Best time to View:
March–April and September–October

Renowned Italian scientist Galileo Galilei gave this phenomenon its Latin name. Aurora was the name of the Roman Goddess of dawn.

Grand Canyon

What and Where:
A deep chasm in Arizona, USA that is 277 miles (445km) long and up to 18 miles (29km) wide in places.
Best Time to View:
All year round

The Grand Canyon was formed by the Colorado River and took 3,600,000 years to form. The river continues to erode and shape the canyon.

Victoria Falls

What and Where:
Victoria Falls is the largest waterfall (based on width and height) in the world. Located in South Africa on the border between Zimbabwe and Zambia, and fed water direct from the Zambezi River, the waterfall is 1, 700 meters (1.7 km) wide and 108 meters (36oft) high.
Best Time to View:
May–October (the dry season)

Dr David Livingstone, a now-famous Scottish explorer, gave the falls their name. It is also known locally as Mosi-oa-Tunya, *which translates as 'smoke that thunders'.*

Mount Everest

What and Where:
Mount Everest is the highest mountain above sea level in the world and is located in the Himalaya Mountains near the Nepal and Tibet, China border. It's peak stands at 8, 848 metres (29,029 ft). The mountain was formed 60, 000, 000 years ago.
Best Time to View:
October–November (when it's less likely to snow)

In 1865, the mountain was named Everest after Sir George Everest, the British Surveyor General of India. Tibetans know the mountain as 'Chomolungma'.

Great Barrier Reef

What and Where:
The world's largest coral reef, situated off North-eastern Australia (Queensland). The reef stretches over 1,600 miles (2,600km) and its 2,900 separate reefs is home to over an estimated 1,500,000,000 fish.
Best Time to View:
June–October – summer.

With over 2,000,000 tourists visiting the reef each year, it is one of the most visited natural environments on Earth.

Harbour of Rio de Janeiro

What and Where:
Also known as Guanabara Bay, the Harbour of Rio de Janeiro is found on the east coast of Brazil. It is the largest bay in the world when based on water volume.
Best Time to View:
September–October

The harbour is 19 miles (31kms) long and 17 miles (28 kilometres) wide at its widest point. The harbour was formed by the erosion from the Atlantic Ocean and is surrounded by extremely unique mountain formations.

Chapter 03.0 **The Living Earth_**

Life As We Used To Know It_

What came first, the chicken or the egg?

It is the eternal question. One moment there was no life, the next there was. A miracle – perhaps. An accident of **a trillion coincidences** coming together to ignite the living world – probably.

Current theories indicate that the conditions that allowed life to begin are no longer present because the life created then has evolved, as has the atmosphere, and any such equivalent organism would not survive in the present conditions on Earth. It is difficult to replicate the planet as it was before life existed and so it is therefore difficult to prove one way or another precisely how life began.

The predominant theories now all have elements of what is often called **Oparin-Haldane Hypothesis**. Russian biochemist Aleksandr Oparin and British-born geneticist John Haldane worked entirely independently but came up with, in essence, the same idea – that life began in a **'primordial soup'** in which organic compounds went through various changes to create more complex molecules.

Something To Think About ...

Prokaryotes are the most primitive cells on the planet but without them no other form of life would exist. In the same way that the longest journey starts with a single step, the journey towards all life on Earth began with the humble prokaryotes.

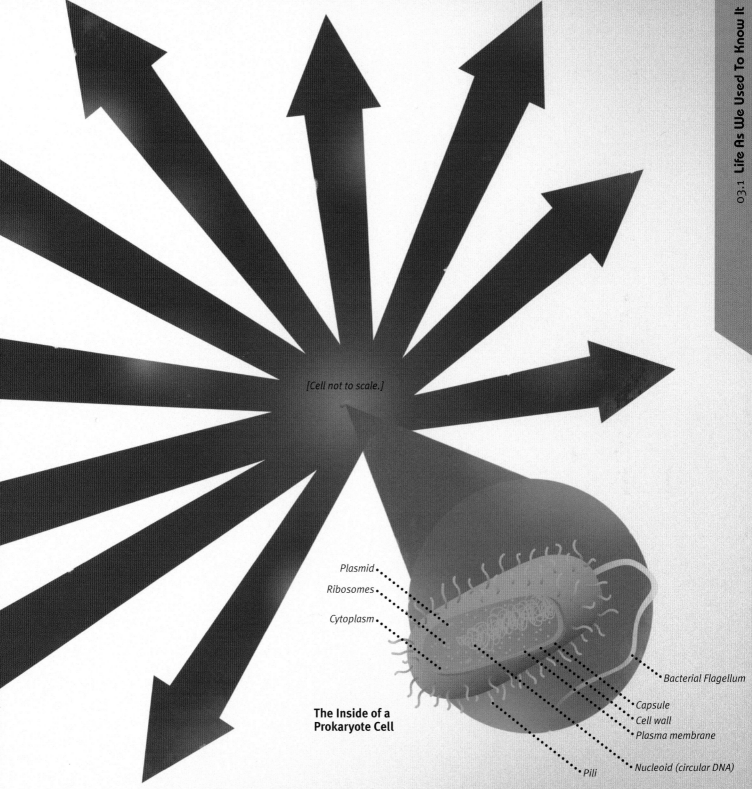

[Cell not to scale.]

Plasmid

Ribosomes

Cytoplasm

Bacterial Flagellum

Capsule

Cell wall

Plasma membrane

Nucleoid (circular DNA)

Pili

**The Inside of a
Prokaryote Cell**

And Then There Were Cells_

As you can see from this timeline, while it took nearly three billion years to go from **simple prokaryotes to multi-cellular life**, it took just a third of that time to go from that to Man. Each successive step on the timeline displayed on this page is as significant as the previous one, but happens much, *much* quicker.

Let's concentrate on the main 'jumps' that led to us – *Homo sapiens*.

1. Simple Cells – prokaryotes
The first living thing and the building block for everything since. Born in a primordial soupy broth.

2. Photosynthesis
Without this, the planet would not have developed its beautifully balanced environment.

3. Ozone layer
The formulation of this created a shield from the Sun's ultraviolet light and made the planet habitable. It is from this moment on that the planet suddenly (sudden being a relative term) becomes populated by living things.

4. Death of the dinosaurs
With dinosaurs around it is unlikely Man would have come along.

5. Genus *Homo*
The first appearance of the genus *Homo* evolve out of *Australopithecus* – the final precursor before *Homo*. This is the last major change on the journey to Man.

3.8 billion years of simple cells (prokaryotes)

3 billion years of photosynthesis

There are two types of primary cells – Eurokaryotic and Prokaryotic. Eurokaryotic cells have a nucleus. Animals, plants and fungi are made up of eurokaryotic cells. Bacteria, which make up 95% of all cells found in the body, are made out of prokaryotic cells.

- 2 billion years of complex cells (eukaryotes)
- 1 billion years of multicellular life
- 600 million years of simple animals
- 570 million years of arthropods (ancestors of insects, arachnids and crustaceans)
- 550 million years of complex animals
- 500 million years of fish and proto-amphibians
- 475 million years of land plants
- 400 million years of insects and seeds
- 360 million years of amphibians
- 300 million years of reptiles
- 200 million years of mammals
- 150 million years of birds
- 130 million years of flowers
- 65 million years since the non-avian dinosaurs died out
- 2.5 million years since the appearance of the genus Homo
- 200,000 years since humans started looking like they do today
- 25,000 years since Neanderthals died out

Photosynthesis_

The process of photosynthesis is vital to life on Earth – taking in carbon dioxide and converting it into oxygen.

To explain this process in plants there is a complex equation:

$6CO_2 + 6H_2o$ Energy from sunlight produces $C_6H_{12}O_6 + 6O_2$

But in effect it is actually quite straightforward:

Carbon Dioxide + Water + Energy from sunlight produces Sugar + Oxygen

Photosynthesis is important because it is the only process by which food is produced from the Sun's energy. This leads directly to all the benefits that the plants provide us with, and without it, we would not be here.

Something To Think About …

Plants are only really concerned with the production of sugar in the process of photosynthesis. The oxygen that occurs as a result of this is, in fact, a waste product and that is why they just release it in to the air.

The energy for photosynthesis comes from light

Plants conduct photosynthesis in specialised cells called chloroplasts

Light energy

Oxygen

Carbon dioxide enters the leaves through tiny holes, or stomata

Carbon Dioxide

Water

The oxygen atoms from the water molecules form oxygen gas molecules

Light energy is converted into chemical energy by chlorophyll – a pigment that energises electrons using specific wavelengths of light. Chlorophyll is also what gives all plants their green colours.

$$C_6H_{12}O_6 + 6O_2$$

03.4 Life Cycle of a Tree_

As well as the vital role they play in producing oxygen for us to breathe, trees – and their wood – have many uses that are equally as important to humans and animals. Trees are used for many of the basic requirements needed for a comfortable existence:

Warmth – wood is a principal material used for making fires.

Cooking – fires provide a method of cooking and heating water.

Shelter – wood was once the main material for house building all over the world and in many developing places it still is. However, since the invention of strong metals, wood plays a reduced part in the construction of houses. But even in countries where wood is not the main component it is still used as part of a building's structure. Trees also play a vital part in animal habitats providing a living environment for many animals, birds and insects.

Transport – almost all early methods of transport relied on wood, especially covering the distances between landmasses across the oceans.

Furniture – every house contains something made of wood, be it a chair, a table or maybe just a fruit bowl.

Communication – the invention of the printing press in 1440 played an important part in enabling better communication around the world but without paper, which is of course made from wood, it would have been impossible to spread the word.

Something To Think About ...

An acorn that falls to the ground has around a 1 in 10,000 chance of developing into a mature oak tree.

A tree reaches its most productive
carbon storage at age ten.

4) Maturation

If luck is still on its side, the seedling
will become a fully-fledged oak tree
and will flower. Oak trees can live
as long as 500 years.

3) Sapling

From becoming a seedling the
green stem will harden and develop
more woody features. Leaves appear
and search for the light.

5) Flowering

Oaks are not pollinated by
insects but by the wind carrying
the pollen. The flowers are not
especially colourful.

6) Fruit

The fruit of the Oak tree is
its seed, the Acorn. The tree
will produce acorns when it
is about 30 years old.

2) Germination

If an acorn avoids being eaten
or destroyed in some other way
it will send down a root and become
a seedling. In the right soil and
conditions the root will have grown
5 inches within a month.

The cycle starts over ...

1) Acorn

This is the seed of the Oak Tree.
It falls from the tree. It is scattered
by animals, particularly squirrels.
Acorns that they drop or don't
get round to eating may
then germinate.

The death of a 70 year old tree releases
three tons of carbon back into the atmosphere.

The Kingdom Of Insects_

Insects are an important part of the **planet's eco-system** and with over a million named and identified species they outnumber all other groups of living creatures. Not only can they be found everywhere, insects are often the only things that can survive in some of the **world's harshest environments**.

Because of their relative size, one of the insect's main functions is to be at the bottom of the food chain, but it would be unfair to think of them simply as a **source of nutrition** for everything else. Insects play an essential role in allowing the flora to flourish by **pollinating** trees and flowers, aerating the soil, and helping dead animals and plants to decompose, thereby **introducing nutrients** into the soil. They also fertilise soil with their own waste and control each other's numbers for the eventual benefit of plant life.

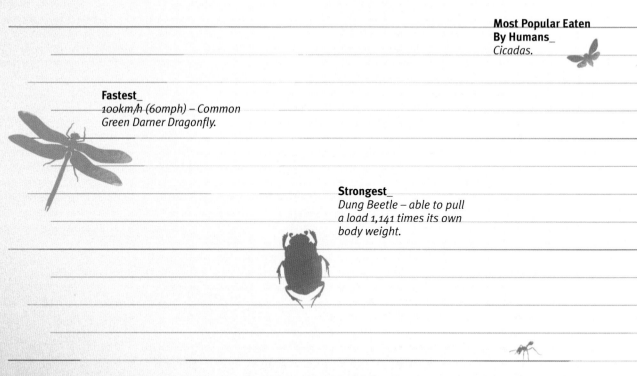

Most Popular Eaten By Humans_
Cicadas.

Fastest_
100km/h (60mph) – Common Green Darner Dragonfly.

Strongest_
Dung Beetle – able to pull a load 1,141 times its own body weight.

Most Toxic Venom_
Pogonomyrmex Ant.

Something To Think About ...

One urban myth states that humans swallow up to eight spiders a year in their sleep. No research has been carried out on this but 60% of people think it is true.

Longest_
30cm (12in) – Walking Stick Insect.

Smallest_
0.2–4mm (0.007–0.15in) –
Fairy Fly (a type of wasp).

Heaviest_
70g (2.5 oz)– Giant Weta
(a type of cricket).

03.6 The Kingdom Of Mammals_

Mammals were present on Earth during the age of the dinosaurs but it was only after the dinosaurs became extinct that these **warm-blooded creatures** – from which human beings evolved – really began to diversify.

One of the main factors that led to this 'branching out' was the disintegration of the supercontinent Pangea during the **Mezozoic period** which caused a diaspora of mammals and plants to flourish in different parts of the planet with different climates. This pollination of life around the world took around 65 million years, a long time to humans, but relatively short compared to the age of the planet.

Smallest_
Kitti's Hog-Nosed Bat –
weighs only 2g (0.7 oz).

Heaviest and strongest_
African Bush Elephant –
up to 11 tonnes.

It's A Fact...

The Bering Land Bridge was important in allowing animals that evolved in North America to travel to Asia. The bridge linked what is now called Siberia to Alaska.

Something To Think About ...

Alligators' jaws have an exceptionally strong closing force. However, the best way to avoid being eaten by an alligator is to hold its mouth shut – it has hardly any opening strength.

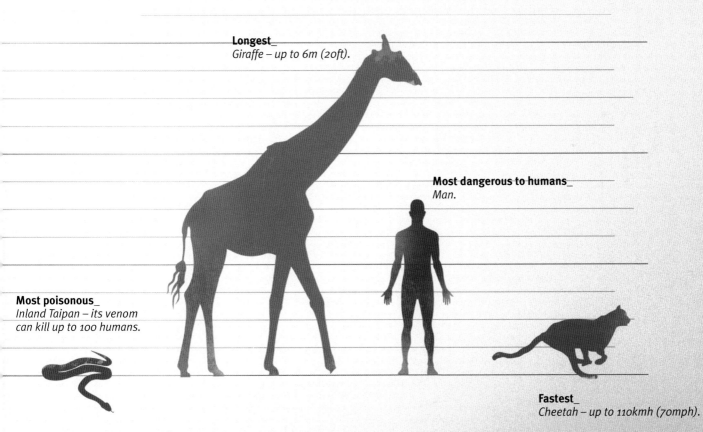

Longest_
Giraffe – up to 6m (20ft).

Most dangerous to humans_
Man.

Most poisonous_
Inland Taipan – its venom can kill up to 100 humans.

Fastest_
Cheetah – up to 110kmh (70mph).

The Kingdom Of The Sea_

Fish, and most ocean-dwelling creatures, have been on Earth since before the dinosaurs, and the **world's first vertebrates** – animals with backbones – were actually jawless fish. This type of fish was not particularly successful, and has left few descendents. This was due to the limitations imposed by their inability to feed due to the lack of a hinged jaw. It is no surprise therefore that fish that did develop a jaw superseded them in the fight for survival. This evolutionary step was vital – it enabled the fish to eat a much greater range of food.

Fish are divided into three classes; **Agnatha** (jawless fish e.g. hagfish), **Chondrichthyes** (cartilaginous fish e.g. sharks) and **Osteichyes** (bony fish e.g. most other fishes). It is from fish, which dominated in the Devonian Period (416–357 million years ago), that land animals first evolved.

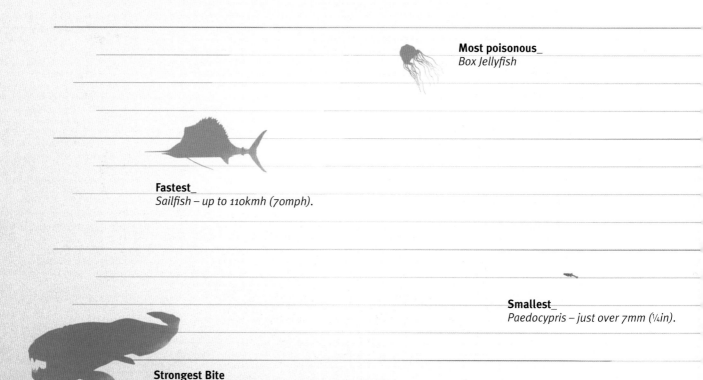

Most poisonous_
Box Jellyfish

Fastest_
Sailfish – up to 110kmh (70mph).

Smallest_
Paedocypris – just over 7mm (¼in).

Strongest Bite
Dunkleosteus terrelli (10m / 30ft) –
Over 1000 lbs force. This fish is extinct.

Something To Think About ...

The number of scales a fish has stays the same throughout its life. It doesn't develop more as it grows, its scales just get bigger.

Most Dangerous to Humans
*Bull Sharks (3.4m / 11 ft) – found
in tropical and
subtropical waters*

Longest and heaviest_
Blue Whale – 33m (108ft), 180 tonnes.

03.8 The Kingdom Of Birds_

Birds are direct descendants of Theropod dinosaurs, the best known of which is *Tyrannosaurus rex*.

The thing that makes birds different from most other vertebrates is their ability to fly. The adaptations which allow flight are an ultra-lightweight skeleton, thanks to hollow bones, exceptionally strong pectoralis muscle and, of course, the aerodynamic shape of the wings.

Fastest flying
*White-throated Needletail
(Spine-tailed Swift) 170kph/105mph*

Heaviest Flying
Kori Bustard – 20kg

Most Dangerous
*Cassowary
Voted the most dangerous bird
on the planet by the Guinness
Book of World Records in 2007*

Most Eaten
*Chicken
Per kilogram per capita,
Hong Kong is the world's
largest consumer of the
humble chicken*

Something To Think About ...

Flamingos are pink because of their food, which is rich in carotene – the same substance that gives carrots their colour.

Biggest Flying Bird
Wandering Albatross – Largest wingspan – Over 3.35m /11ft

Heaviest, Tallest and Strongest
Ostrich 3m (10ft) / 160kg (353lb)

Smallest
Bee Hummingbird 5cm (2in) / 3g (1/12 oz)

The Age Of Dinosaurs_

03.9

When did dinosaurs rule the Earth ... and for how long?

The first dinosaurs appeared during the **Triassic Period**, 210–250 million years ago (mya) when Earth had just one super continent Pangea. Their peak, when they dominated the planet, was the **Jurassic Period**, 150–210 mya. At this time, the continent was beginning to break up and the **Cretaceous Period** (65–150 mya) saw the distribution of the landmass beginning to resemble what we now have. Towards the end of this period the most famous and fiercest dinosaur, the *Tyrannosaurus rex*, ruled the roost – but was not the *biggest* dinosaur, contrary to popular myth. A Sauropod, called an Argetinosaurus – weighing in at 100 tons and 120ft tall – takes the prize of the biggest dinosaur found so far.

What was the gap between us and them? We, that is *Homo sapiens*, appeared about 250,000 years ago.

Triassic Period
210–250 mya
(Eoraptor, Coelophysis and Herrerasaurus)

Jurassic Period
150–210 mya
(Brachiosaurus, Scelidosaurus, Dilophosaurus

82

Something To Think About ...

At present over 700 different species of dinosaurs have been discovered, identified and named. However, paleontologists are certain that there are many more species (and the fossils they have left behind) still to be discovered. Let's hope we find them before it's too late.

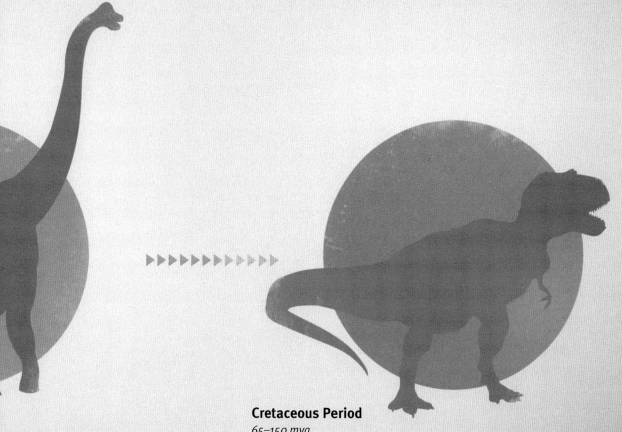

Cretaceous Period
65–150 mya
(Tyrannosaurus, Ornithomimus, Triceratops)

What Killed The Dinosaurs?

The **K-T Boundary** is the point on the pre-historic timeline that indicates when the dinosaurs disappeared. This boundary refers to the periods either side of the line '**K**' (for Cretaceous) and '**T**' (for Tertiary). Fossil records show the existence of dinosaurs on the K side of the boundary but not on the T side (providing we ignore birds, of course, which are direct descendants of dinosaurs).

The ongoing scientific debate revolves not around the fact that Earth's climate changed dramatically, and suddenly, 65 million years ago (thus destroying the atmosphere and environment vital for dinosaur survival) but why the climate changed so drastically. What happened to Earth for everything to change *so* fast?

The most common, and established, theory to answer this question was proposed by Walter Alvarez and his team of geologists in 1980. Alvarez stated that an asteroid had hit Earth, instantly killing everything within a 480-km (300-mile) radius, throwing a huge amount of debris up into the atmosphere. This debris quickly blocked out the Sun, causing the temperature to drop, and led to the rapid extinction of the dinosaurs and **75% of all living species** that inhabited Earth.

Something To Think About ...

There are two reasons we want to know what happened to the dinosaurs. First we're just interested, it is just this type of curiosity that has pushed Mankind to great heights. Second, and probably more importantly, if something could wipe dinosaurs off the face of the planet, couldn't the same happen to us? If so, wouldn't it be good to work out what that something is before it happens again?

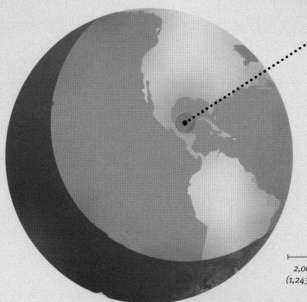

Dinosaur Killer

When: 65,000,000 years ago (65 mya)
Location: Chicxulub, Yucatan Peninsula, Mexico
Size of crater: 180km (112 miles)
Size of asteroid: 10km (6 miles) in diameter
Size of explosion (in energy): 2,000,000 times the biggest thermonuclear bomb or 100,000,000 megatons of TNT
Level of destruction: 75% of all species on Earth wiped out

2,000km
(1,243 miles)

A comparative study of the impact of the asteroid that killed off the dinosaurs 65, 000, 000 years ago and 1945's Hiroshima bomb – mankind's worst example of destruction.

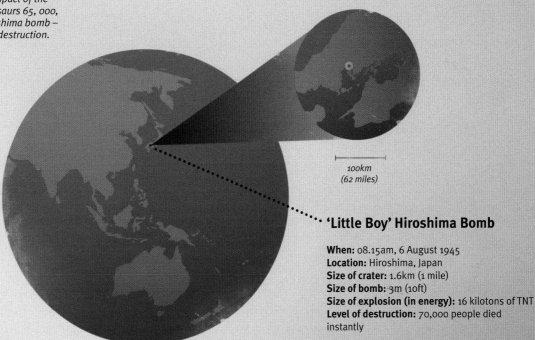

100km
(62 miles)

'Little Boy' Hiroshima Bomb

When: 08.15am, 6 August 1945
Location: Hiroshima, Japan
Size of crater: 1.6km (1 mile)
Size of bomb: 3m (10ft)
Size of explosion (in energy): 16 kilotons of TNT
Level of destruction: 70,000 people died instantly

The Food Chain_

The food chain is an easy way of looking at the movement and direction of food (thus providing the energy to live) from one animal to another within an environment or animal habitat. The food chain is a vital part of an ecosystem and shows how the survival of one species is always connected closely with the survival of others.

No matter what food chain we begin with, we always start with the **Primary Producer** – the lowest level on the chain (i.e. the first to be eaten). The position occupied on the chain is referred to as the **Trophic Level**. The Primary Producer is at level one.

For instance, in a food chain beginning with grass (Primary Producer) the next trophic level up would be the grasshopper (**Primary Consumer**). The grasshopper is then eaten by a lizard as the **Secondary Consumer**. The lizard will then be eaten by a **Tertiary Consumer** and so on. Many organisms and animals may assume different trophic levels on different food chains.

The balance of the planet's ecosystems depends on keeping all levels of these chains constantly supplied. If there is a shortfall at any level there will be repercussions all the way up, and down, the chain. If there are not enough producers to supply the consumer, then the consumers will die off. If a consumer dies out, a producer may become too dominant and kill off its producer, and so on.

Many food chains around the world are currently threatened by the destruction of animal habitats such as rainforests.

Something To Think About ...

Those at the top of a food chain are called Apex Predators. Humans are the most obvious example, but others include whales, tigers and eagles.

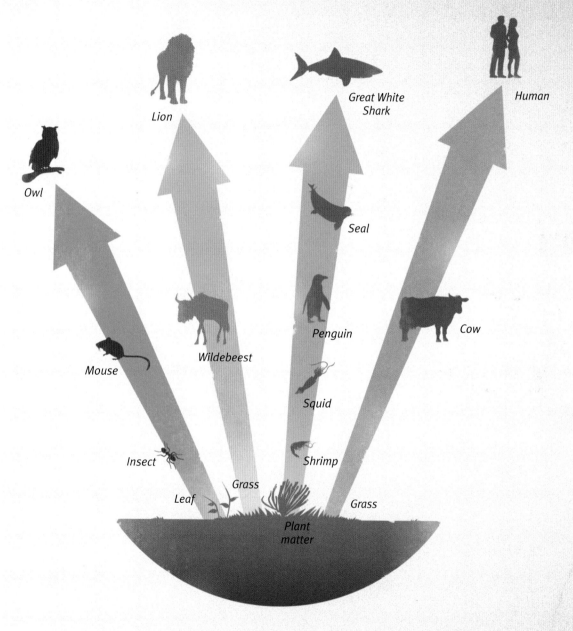

Owl

Lion

Great White
Shark

Human

Seal

Mouse

Penguin

Cow

Wildebeest

Squid

Insect

Shrimp

Grass

Leaf

Grass

Plant
matter

At each level, energy is passed on to the consumer but there is always energy lost.
In fact less than 15% of energy is passed on at each level.

03.12 Lifespan of Animals_

Daniel Defoe was probably the first writer to highlight that there are two certainties in life: death and taxes. What we don't know is when the former will come along.

All living things are born and then at some time later they die ... but the gap in between varies enormously from one organism to another. A mayfly, for example, can have a lifespan as short as 30 minutes whilst the Giant Tortoise can expect to be around for over 150 years. In the plant world the Bristlecone Pine can live to an incredible 5,000 years.

Jeanne Calment has the **longest confirmed human lifespan**. She was born, in Arles, France, on 21 February 1875 and died, 122 years later, on 4 August 1997.

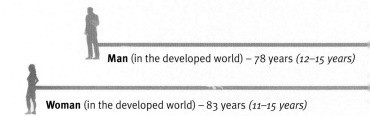

Man (in the developed world) – 78 years *(12–15 years)*

Woman (in the developed world) – 83 years *(11–15 years)*

Something To Think About ...

The plastic collar of a four-pack of cans will outlive us all – with a lifespan of over 400 years. This is, coincidentally, 399 years and 361 days longer than the actual four-pack of drink is expected to last.

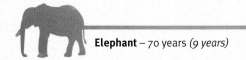

Elephant – 70 years *(9 years)*

Mouse – 4 years *(35 days females; 60 days males)*

Crocodile – 45 years *(16 years male, 13 years female)*

Camel – 50 years *(5 years)*

Queen Bee – 3 years *(5–7 days)*

Sheep – 15 years *(6–8 months)*

Horse – 40 years *(1–2 years)*

Tarantula – 15 years *(2 years)*

Gerbil – 5 years *(9–12 weeks)*

Kangaroo – 9 years *(22 months)*

Dog – 15 years *(6–12 months)*

Man (Swaziland, Africa) – 39.8 years *(lowest on the United Nations list of life expectancy)*

Canary – 24 years *(5 months)*

Cat – 15–20 years *(7–12 months)*

Lion – 35 years *(3–5 years)*

[Figures in brackets indicate when the species becomes sexually active.]

Chapter 04.0 **Humans_**

The Evolution Of Man From Monkey_

Like monkeys, apes and even lemurs, human beings are classed as **Primates** – the first of which appeared around 65 million years ago (mya), after the dinosaurs had died out and Earth's climate had stabilised once again. Whilst we could trace our evolution further back in history, this particular moment in time was really the start of our own distinct branch of evolution.

Fifteen million years after primates first appeared, *Hominidae* (or Great Ape) evolved, but it was still another ten million years before the emergence of the earliest known primate that displayed distinct elements of Man. The proof of this is a fossil dating from around 4.5 mya that shows *Ardipithecus ramidus* to be predominantly bi-pedal (two-legged). He was followed (3–4 mya) by *Australopithecus anamensis* and *Australopithecus afarensis*, both showing signs of permanent bi-pedalism. The brain at this evolutionary step was still small, and facial features were still mainly ape-like, but the teeth were gradually becoming smaller.

Something To Think About ...

It is believed that toward the end of the late Pleistocene period, about 75,000 years ago, the number of *Homo sapiens sapiens* got as low as 1,000 breeding couples, and it is from this small group that we all come.

The Neanderthal was as strong, intelligent and resourceful as sapiens, but around 30,000 years ago they became extinct, while *Homo sapiens* flourished and eventually became *Homo sapiens sapiens* – that's us.

Homo erectus came next around 1.8 mya. His facial features are now closer to human than ape, body hair has greatly reduced and brain size is about three-quarters that of a modern human's.

Fossil remains have been found of *habilis* along with primitive tools. Standing around 1.5m (5ft tall), *habilis* had a brain cavity big enough to house an organ capable of primitive speech.

Over the next two million years evolution began to speed up with three further species of *Australopithecus*: *africanus*, *robustus* and, finally, *boisei* around one million years ago. These overlap with the appearance, at last, of *Homo*, about 2.5 mya, in the shape of *Homo habilis*.

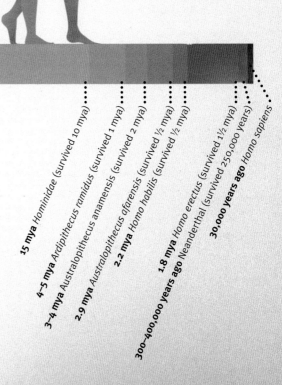

65 mya *First primates (survived 50 mya)*

15 mya *Hominidae (survived 10 mya)*

4–5 mya *Ardipithecus ramidus (survived 1 mya)*

3–4 mya *Australopithecus anamensis (survived 2 mya)*

2.9 mya *Australopithecus afarensis (survived ½ mya)*

2.2 mya *Homo habilis (survived ½ mya)*

1.8 mya *Homo erectus (survived 1½ mya)*

300–400,000 years ago *Neanderthal (survived 250,000 years)*

30,000 years ago *Homo sapiens*

Human Composition_

What is the recipe for a human?

Most people know that we're mostly made up of water – on average, around 60% of our body weight. But where do we keep it and why don't we drip everywhere?

Most of it is **intracellular fluid**, meaning that it is contained within the living cells of the body. Our blood only represents around 5% of our total body weight. Of the remaining 40% of body weight, around 18% is made up of **fat**, 15% **protein** and the remaining 7% **mineral**, mainly in the form of **bone**.

Something To Think About ...

The human body is a miracle. But we take it for granted. In order for it to carry out the simplest of instructions, or what we assume are simple, our brain must orchestrate and utilise many different muscles – as well as express many differing emotions – at the same time. Reading this sentence for example involves the complex movement of many eye muscles straining together, the coordination of the relevant brain centres in interpreting the meaning and then deciphering how it makes you feel.

Average time between blinks of the eyes =
2.8 seconds

Potassium *0.35%*

Phosphorus *1.1%*

Calcium *2%*

Nitrogen *3%*

Carbon *18%*

Total number of human taste buds =
10,000

Oxygen *65%*

There are 2.5 trillion red blood cells in your body
at any moment in time. Your body creates
2, 500, 000 every second.

Number of receptor cells in your nose =
12 million (a dog has 1 billion!)

Hydrogen *10%*

Sulphur *0.25%*

Chlorine *0.15%*

Sodium *0.15%*

Magnesium, iron, manganese,
copper, iodine, cobalt, zinc
traces

04.3 Deoxyribonucleic Acid (DNA)_

Deoxyribonucleic acid or, as it is most commonly referred to, DNA, holds all the **genetic information** of all living things. Although it was first discovered by Swiss scientist, Friedrich Miescher in 1871, it was an American, James D. Watson, and a Briton, Francis Crick, who in 1953 first correctly modelled the **double-helix** structure which makes up what we recognise as DNA.

The DNA that we are made up of individually is inherited from our parents and it is the information held in this passed on DNA that means that we take on separate elements of both parents. The mix will always vary which is why siblings do not look identical, except in the case of identical twins that develop from the same egg, and therefore from exactly the same combination of **chromosomes**.

99.9% of DNA is identical across all humans. However, the 0.1% difference is enough to distinguish one person's look, features and personality from another – it is this that makes you *you*. It is this 0.1% that has allowed **genetic fingerprinting** to be used by police to find criminals, or discount the innocent.

Something To Think About ...

Because everything on the planet originates from the same place, most likely the Big Bang, we share elements of our DNA with everything. For instance 60% of our DNA is the same as a banana.

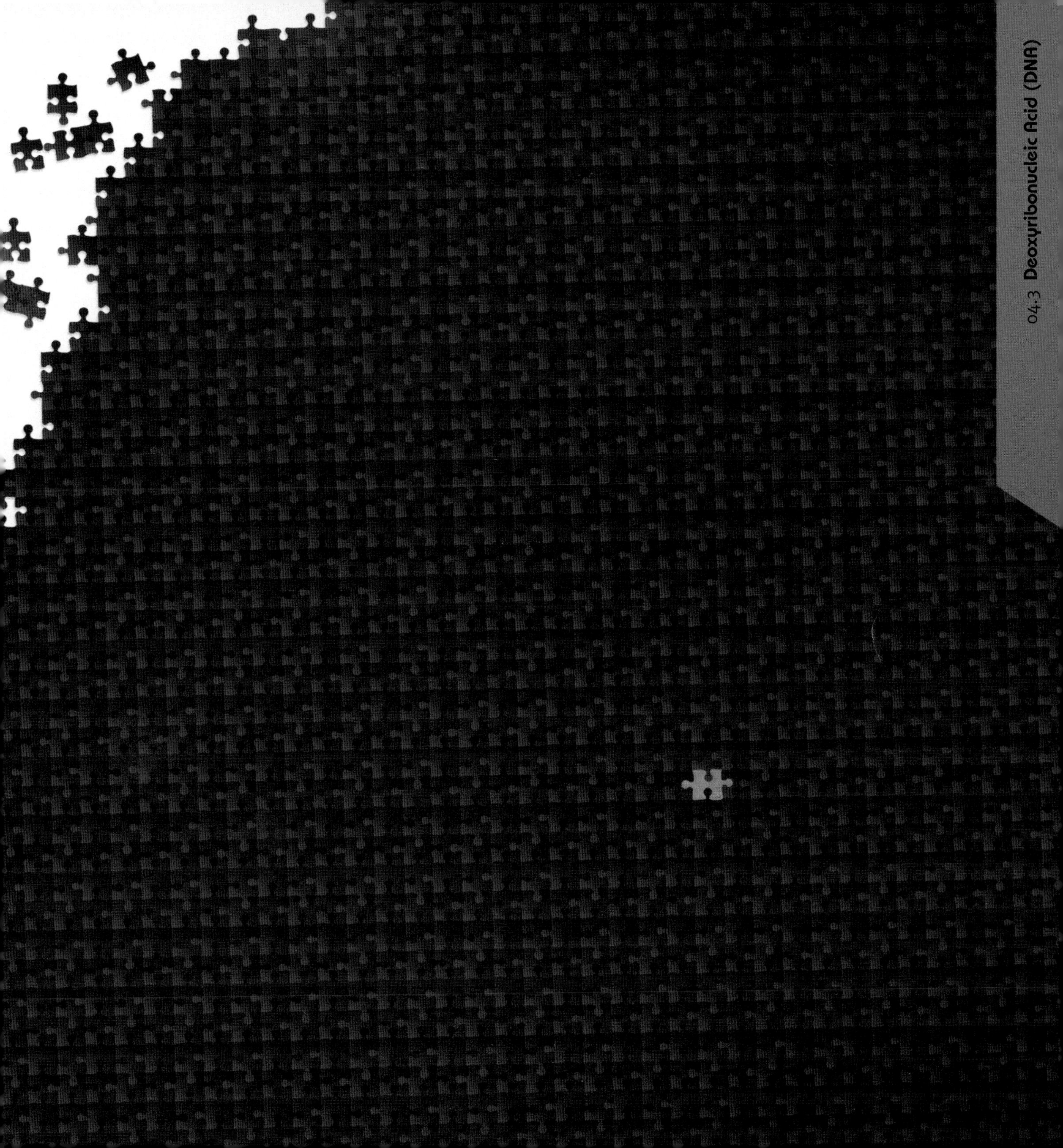

04.4 The Brain_

Our brain is the centre of everything we are. It holds our memories, controls all our functions, enables us to live, and most importantly, think. When Man learnt to use fire, and started cooking meat, the amount of blood used to digest food was reduced. This excess blood allowed the brain to grow in size, evolve and develop thereby enabling us to move ahead of the pack.

The brain comprises three main parts: the **cerebral cortex**, the **cerebellum** and the **brain stem**. The cerebral cortex is further split into four lobes: **frontal**, **parietal**, **temporal** and **occipital**. These lobes are connected, and made up of, **neurons** and **glia**. The neurons do the donkeywork of sending electric signals around the body, whilst the glia acts as a bodyguard for the neurons, protecting and nourishing them.

Much of the research into the brain, and identifying which parts are responsible for which function, is based on monitoring behaviour when certain parts of the brain are injured, or even removed.

Something To Think About ...

The brain weighs around 1.4kg (3lb) which, as a percentage of body weight, it is the biggest brain on the planet. There are 100 billion neurons in the brain. It is 78% water, 11% lipids, 8% protein, 1% carbohydrate, 2% other stuff. It is difficult to calculate the storage space in the brain but some estimates have it as high as 1000 terabytes.

Cerebral Cortex

Parietal lobe: *co-ordinates much of the sensory information we receive.*

Frontal lobe: *the decision-making centre and home of our personality and thoughts.*

Occipital lobe: *the core of our visual perception.*

Cerebellum ·

Receives information regarding movement, refines it, and sends the signals onto the relevant parts of the body. Less understood is the part it plays in thought processes.

Temporal lobe: *co-ordinates sensory information, mainly audio, also important in speech. Contains the* hippocampus *which is central to long term memory.*

Brain Stem

Vital in that it connects the brain to the rest of the body. Lower half is the medulla oblongata *that looks after unconscious activity such as breathing and heart beat.*

Total number of neurons in the brain = 100 billion

04.5 Skeleton And Muscles_

Whilst research into the human brain is still in its infancy, our knowledge of the body is incredibly advanced.

An adult human has **206 bones**, and together these form the **skeleton**, within, on and around which everything else in the human body is organised. Our vital organs are held within the protective confines of the **ribcage**, our brain is protected within the **skull** and we are covered in a protective layer, the outer-most part of which is the **skin**.

We have between 600 and 800 muscles in our body and these fall into three types: **skeletal**, **smooth** and **cardiac**. The first of these, skeletal muscles, are connected to our bones and used for motion. We consciously control these actions. Smooth muscles make up the walls of organs such as the bladder and stomach. These muscles operate automatically without us having to instruct them. Finally there is the cardiac muscle, the **heart**. This is the only muscle that never rests, and its job is to pump blood around the body.

Something To Think About ...

Babies have over 300 bones and much more cartilage than adults. As they mature the cartilage ossifies into bone, and thus some of their bones are fused, resulting in the 206 bones present in the body of a fully mature adult.

Muscles of the body / Bones of the Body

Frontalis • • • • • • • • • • • • • • • • • Skull

Orbicularis oris *(circular muscle of the eyelids)* • • • • • • • • • • • • • Frontal bone *(forehead)*

Zygoma *(cheek bone)*

Maxilla *(upper/lower jaw)*

Sternocleidomastoids *(neck)* • • • • • • • •

Trapezius *(back, spine support)* • • • • • • • • • • • •

Deltoids *(triangular shoulder muscles)* • • • • • • • • • • • Clavicle *(collarbone)*

Pectorals *(chest)* • • • • • • • • • • • • • •

The Heart • • • • • • • • • • • • •

Triceps *(back, upper arms)* • • • • • • • • • • Humerus *(Upper arm)*

Biceps *(arm muscle with two points of attachment)* • • • • • • • • •

Latissimus dorsi *(back muscle)* • • • • • • • • • • •

Rectus Abdominus *(stomach)* • • • • • • • • • Ulna *(lesser forearm bone)*

Radius *(main forearm bone)*

Carpals *(wrist bones)*

Illum, pubis, ischium *(pelvic bones)*

Gluteus maximus *(buttocks)* • • • • • • • • • • • • •

Sartorius *(thigh, longest muscle in the body)* • • • • • • • • • • • • •

Hamstrings *(back, thighs)* • • • • • • • • • • • • •

Quadriceps *(front thigh)* • • • • • • • • • • • Femur *(thigh bone)*

Patella *(kneecap)*

Tibia *(main shinbone)*

Gastrocnemius *(two calf muscles)* • • • • • • • • • • • • • • Fibula *(calf bone)*

Achilles Tendon *(back, attaches calf to heel)* • • • • • • • • • •

Tarsals *(ankle bones)*

Metatarsals *(foot bones)*

Phalanges *(toe bones)*

Calcaneus *(heel)*

The Senses_

The importance of the head, skull and brain is demonstrated by the fact that **four of the five senses** are housed and operated solely within that area. Touch is the odd one out but is still controlled by the brain that processes the pressure signals that come from all over the body.

Humans are predominantly visual creatures. We are able to see things because **light enters our eye** and is focussed onto the **retina** at the back of the eyeball. The cells in the retina convert this information into **electrical signals,** which are sent to the brain to interpret. Different cells in the retina deal with colour and brightness.

Sound waves make the **eardrum** vibrate. These vibrations are passed onto the cochlea, within which are hair cells that generate a nerve impulse that is sent to the brain.

Taste begins when the buds, mainly on the tongue, are stimulated. There are five **receptors** that can detect **sweet, sour, bitter, salty,** and **umami.** Umami is a savoury taste that was discovered as recently as 1908 due to it being the most subtle of the five tastes. Indeed, many people do not even realise it exists.

Smell is closely related to taste and each can be affected by the loss of the other. It is triggered by the stimulation of **olfactory receptors** in the nose. There are many more smell receptors than taste.

We perceive **touch** through the **receptors on our skin,** including the tiny hairs with which it is covered. The receptors vary in sensitivity depending on where they are on the body so, for example, the palm of your hand is more sensitive to touch than the back of your hand.

Something To Think About ...

We all have a blind spot where the optic nerve passes through the retina. Cover your left eye and look at the O from about 20cm (8in) from this book. Slowly move away and the X will disappear.

O   **X**

Each time you blink your eyes are shut for 0.3 seconds. That means your eyes are shut for 30 minutes of each day just through blinking.

A newborn baby initially sees the world upside down because it takes time for a baby's brain to turn the picture the right way up.

Your nose can tell the difference between 4,000 and 10,000 smells. The older you are, the fewer amount of smells you can detect.

75% *of all sensory processes in the brain are* **Visual**

12% *of all sensory processes in the brain involve* **Smell, Taste and Touch**

13% *of all sensory processes in the brain involve* **Hearing**

Taste is the weakest of the five senses.

Scientists measure loudness in decibels. A whisper is 20 decibels, car traffic is 70 decibels and a gun shot is 140 decibels.

Where Your Organs Are_

In the trunk of the human body, protected by the ribcage, are the **main organs** – everything but the brain. The most important of these organs is the **heart** as it is this engine that pumps vital, **oxygen-enriched blood** all around the body and makes everything else work.

The oxygen carried in the blood is first processed by the **lungs**. Fresh oxygen is inhaled by breathing causing our lungs to expand. The oxygen in this air binds to the **haemoglobin** in the red blood cells, which then release their carbon dioxide. This carbon dioxide is expelled as the lungs contract.

The **kidneys** play an important role in keeping the blood clean. They process about 165 litres (36 gallons) every day. The waste products and excess fluids are expelled as urine via the bladder.

The **liver** has many functions, the main one of which is the production of bile to help **food digestion**. It also helps to keep the blood clean by disposing of worn-out red blood cells.

The **intestine**, split into small and large, processes food and extracts the protein, fats, carbohydrates and vitamins. The small intestine is about 6m (20ft) long, whilst the large is only 1.5m (5ft).

Something To Think About ...

Whilst our breathing happens subconsciously a dolphin has to make a conscious decision to take each breath.

Brain
Controls your body and mind

Lungs
Mixes blood with oxygen, disposes of used air and carbon dioxide

Lungs

Heart
Circulates blood throughout body

Liver
Breaks down toxins into less poisonous compounds and creates proteins and amino acids

Stomach
Receives food, stores it, then empties it into the duodenum

Spleen
Filters, stores and cleans blood

Gallbladder
Stores bile for digestion

Pancreas
Secretes digestive enzymes to control blood sugar levels

Kidney
Makes urine from waste products and excess water in blood

Kidney

Large intestine
Converts food products into faeces

Small intestine
Chemically digests food and helps absorb nutrients into blood system

Appendix
Unknown function

Bladder
Stores urine

Skin
Protects body from infection, damage and drying out

04.8 The Cycle Of Life_

The primary purpose of all living things is to guarantee the continuation of their species. We do this by **sexual reproduction**.

Sexual reproduction is the combination, or joining together, of **gametes**. In humans this is a **sperm** (from the male) and an **egg** (from the female). Together they create a new cell called a **zygote**.

Each gamete contains one set of **chromosomes**, whilst the new cell, the zygote, contains two sets – one from each parent. It is in these chromosomes that the genetic material from the parents is passed on to the infant.

The male reproductive system is made up of two parts: the **penis and the testicles**. The latter produces the **sperm**, whilst the former delivers it. Sperm does not survive for long and so men have to produce them constantly.

The female reproductive system comprises the **vagina and uterus,** and the **ovaries**. The ovaries produce the egg and it is in the uterus that the sperm and egg combine.

Something To Think About…

Before sexual reproduction, cells just made copies of themselves. This meant that evolution only occurred when mistakes in the copying process were made. Sexual reproduction was a vital factor in speeding up evolution.

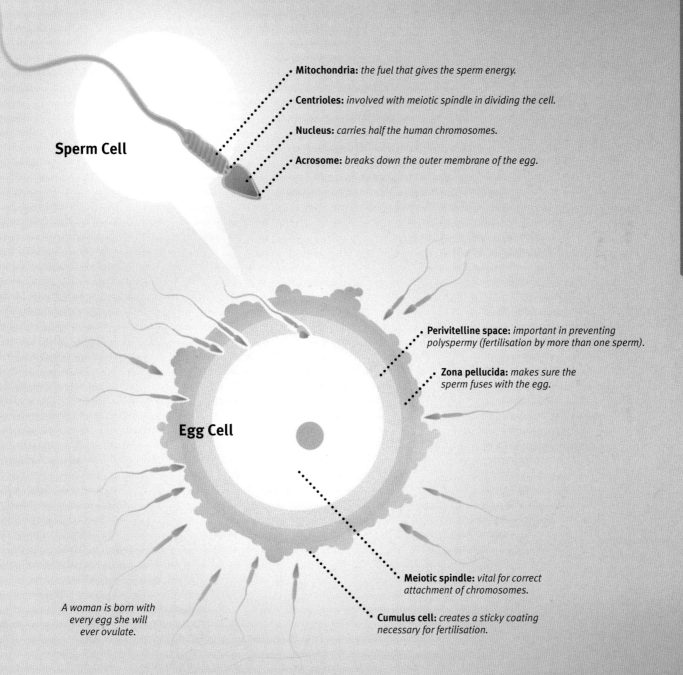

Sperm Cell

Mitochondria: *the fuel that gives the sperm energy.*

Centrioles: *involved with meiotic spindle in dividing the cell.*

Nucleus: *carries half the human chromosomes.*

Acrosome: *breaks down the outer membrane of the egg.*

Egg Cell

Perivitelline space: *important in preventing polyspermy (fertilisation by more than one sperm).*

Zona pellucida: *makes sure the sperm fuses with the egg.*

A woman is born with every egg she will ever ovulate.

Meiotic spindle: *vital for correct attachment of chromosomes.*

Cumulus cell: *creates a sticky coating necessary for fertilisation.*

How The Body Works_

As humans evolved and we moved from a hunter-gatherer existence to a more sedentary lifestyle it became necessary for us to be able to digest a wider variety and larger amount of food. Our digestive system evolved hand in hand with this need.

The first stage in the **digestive system** is the teeth and these have changed quite remarkably over time. As our ability to pre-cut food and cook it has improved so have our teeth, helping the stomach to digest smaller, more manageable, pieces of food.

The biggest single leap in the evolution of our digestive system was the discovery of **fire** as a method of cooking meat and vegetables. This process instantly made it much easier for our stomachs to extract the **proteins** from the meat and suddenly gave humans access to nutrients in plants that were impossible to digest without cooking.

There are many systems that control your body. They are:

1. **The Respiratory System** (regulates breathing)
2. **The Cardiovascular System** (regulates blood flow)
3. **The Digestive System** (regulates the processing of food)
4. **The Endocrine System** (regulates the body's hormones)
5. **The Immune System** (regulates the body's protective defence)
6. **The Reproductive System** (regulates sperm/egg/fertilisation production)
7. **The Excretory System** (regulates waste production)
8. **The Nervous System** (regulates neurons)

Something To Think About ...

Whilst controlling fire was vital in cooking, it was also important in allowing human activity to extend beyond the hours of daylight. Suddenly our lives were not ruled by the Sun.

Mouth_
Food enters here and is chewed to aid digestion.

Throat_
Swallowing, a conscious decision, moves the food into the throat.

Oesophagus_
The link to the stomach. The connection is closed off by the lower oesophageal sphincter. This relaxes as food approaches to let it in.

Stomach_
Once the food is here the work really begins. The food is mixed with digestive juices. When this process is complete the stomach releases into the ...

Small intestine_
This is where nutrients, fats and carbohydrates are extracted into juices and passed to the pancreas and liver, whilst the remainder moves onto the ...

Large intestine_
Where final digestion occurs and the remaining bits of useful nutrients are extracted.

What is left after this is pushed into the colon and out past the final sphincter, the anus, as faeces.

Throughout this system our body produces digestive juices to help break down the food into nutrients, starting with saliva, in the mouth, followed by bile, from the liver.

The Development Of Speech_

All animals communicate but humans have – by far – the most sophisticated level of communication, and this is one more factor that has helped us get ahead of the pack.

Our earliest level of communication, during the time of the Great Apes 14 million years ago (mya), was at the same level as modern apes. The first development that allowed us to speak was the switch to **bi-pedalism**. This changed the position of the skull relative to the body and thus elongated the **vocal tract**. This meant we could physically produce a wider variety, and number, of sounds.

Around the time of *Homo ergaster* (2.5 mya) and *Homo heidelbergenis* (600,000 years ago) it is thought that mothers developed a kind of 'baby talk' to comfort their children and this was the first properly vocalised human speech.

The fossil evidence of **advanced tools** that were produced using more than one substance or material is cited as proof of the further development of language and speech. The reasoning behind this is that to pass on the knowledge of those tools' construction there must have been some verbal communication.

One of the biggest leaps in the development of language was the ability to refer to things not in the immediate vicinity, either by time or place. Whilst the teaching of tool-making techniques was important, it is this function both of thought – and of vocalising this thought – which brought our language skills to where we are today.

Taumatawhakatangihangak

Something To Think About ...

Wernicke (towards the back) and **Broca** (near the front) are the two areas of the brain that control speech: wernicke decides what we want to say; broca sends the impulse to the muscles to produce the sounds.

The Longest Words in the World.

Pneumonoultramicroscopicsilicovolcanokoniosis
English (a type of lung disease, 45 letters)

Anticonstitutionnellement
French (meaning 'unconstitutionally', 35 letters)

Rindfleischetikettierungsüberwachungsaufgabenübertragungsgesetz
German (A German Law regarding the labelling of beef, 63 letters)

Nghiêng
Vietnamese (meaning inclined, 7 letters)

ונְיָתוֹידֵפוֹלְקִיצְנָאלְשְׁכּוּ
Hebrew (meaning 'and when to our encyclopedias', 19 letters)

Taumatawhakatangihangakoauauotamateaturipukakapikimaungahoronukupokaiwhenuakitanatahu
Maori (a Maori place name – the longest place name in the world, 85 letters)

ジャリメツノキイワトメヅイネメトビセチキ
Japanese (a name of a sea weed, 21 letters)

Precipitevolissimevolmente
Italian (to precipitate, to be hasty, sudden and rash, 26 letters)

Electroencefalografistas
Spanish (a technician who uses a electroencephalograph, 24 letters)

Dampskipsundervannsstyrkeprøvemaskinerikonstruksjonsvanskeligheter
Norwegian (meaning steamship-underwater-strength-test-machinery-construction-difficulties, 66 letters)

It's A Fact...

Hippopotomonstrosesquipedaliophobia (35 letters) is the fear of long words.

Memory_

If we are who we are because of all the things we experience, then memory is fundamental to what makes us who we *are*. If we have no memory, then we are reborn every second.

The process of remembering has **three** basic stages; **registering**, **storing** and **retrieving**. It is generally felt that we have two main areas of storage: short-term and long-term.

When we register an event, a fact or even just a person's name, **neurons** are stimulated in our brain by the messages received through our senses. When we remember that event, these same neurons are activated in the same way, and the memory is **recalled**. The simplest analogy to remember this process is that of the oldest system used in computers, the punch card.

The difference between **long-term** and **short-term memory** is that for the latter the holes are not punched permanently and it is only by repetition that the holes are retained and moved into the long-term space. The classic example often cited is a phone number. When we are told a number by a friend we can retain that number in our short-term memory just long enough to dial it but unless we repeat it several times it will disappear.

Something To Think About ...

Chunking is a simple way to help remember things – especially numbers. We do this quite naturally with phone numbers when we split them in to chunks in our head. The optimum chunk size is three digits.

Flow chart showing how human memory works.

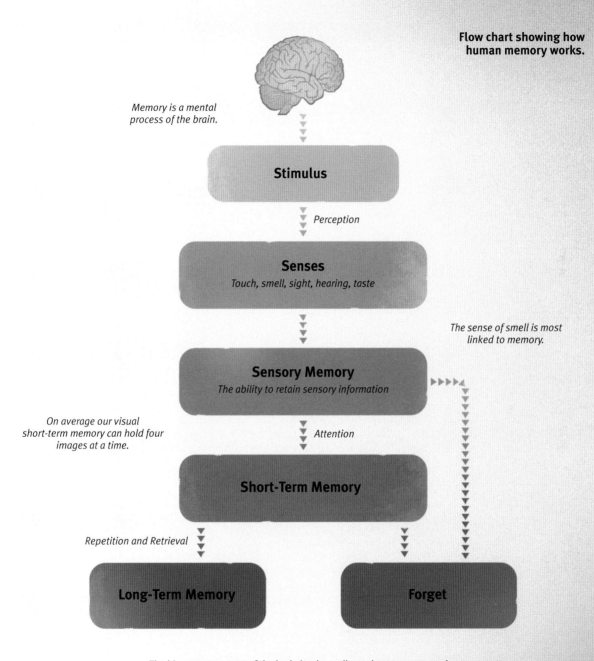

Memory is a mental process of the brain.

Stimulus

Perception

Senses
Touch, smell, sight, hearing, taste

The sense of smell is most linked to memory.

Sensory Memory
The ability to retain sensory information

On average our visual short-term memory can hold four images at a time.

Attention

Short-Term Memory

Repetition and Retrieval

Long-Term Memory

Forget

The hippocampus part of the brain is where all our short-term memories are formed and stored. When someone tells you a telephone number to remember it goes direct to the hippocampus.

04.12 From Fertilisation To Birth_

This timeline details the growth, size and development of a baby in a womb.

Week 1
Fertilisation and **Cell division.**
The size of this dot – .

Week 2
Same size as a drawing pin
150 cells

Three layers **Endoderm** (becomes respiratory and digestive system), **Mesoderm** (bones, circulatory system), **Ectoderm** (brain, nervous system, hair, skin and nails)

Week 4
Same size as a grain of rice
5mm (0.2 in)
Embryo – no longer looks like an egg. Buds for arms and legs appear.

Week 6–8
Same size as a baked bean
9–22mm (1/3–8/10in)/1.5-2g (5/100–7/1000z)
Eyes and ears begin to form as small cavities in the head. Brain cells and lungs are developing rapidly, reflexes are evident, mouth can be opened. Bone forms, all vital organs are present.

Week 9
Same size as a golf ball
5.5cm (2in)/10g (1/3oz)
Mouth can open, eyes are fully formed, heart beating 150 bpm.

Week 11
size as a credit card *Same*
8.5cm (3 1/3in)/30g (1oz)
Vital organs can now function. Foetus can swallow.

Week 12
Same size as a mobile phone
10cm (4in)/45g (1 ½ oz)
Facial muscles work.

Week 13–18
Same size as a dollar bill
12–20cm (4 ¾–7 ¾in)/65–135g (2 ¼–4 ¾oz)
Most body parts and organs formed and in place now; heart beats twice as fast as mother's. Baby can hear, but can't interpret the sounds. It's time to grow...

Week 19–20
Same size as a football
21–23cm (8 ¼–9in)/280–360g (9 ¾–12 ½oz)
Milk teeth begin to form. A waxy coating, vernix, appears – this protects the skin but will dissolve

114

Week 22
Same size as a basketball
26cm (10 ¼in)/480g (16 ¾oz)
White bloods cells, which fight illness, are produced for the first time. Skin is still see through.

Week 23–26
28–32cm (11–12 ½in)/550–740g (19 ½–26oz)
First lines of fingerprints, hearing system now complete. Bones are hardening, baby sucks thumb, and can cry.

Week 27–30
35–37cm (13 ¾–14 1/2in) / 900g–1.4kg (2–3lb)
Eyes can open. If male, testes descend. Music heard now will be remembered. Baby now fills the space available.

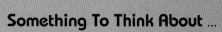

Week 31–35
Same size as a bowling pin
40–45cm (15 ¾–17 ¾in)/1.7–2.3kg (3 ¾–5lb)
Vernix and Lanugo start to disappear, Baby practises breathing. Hair appears on head.

Week 38
50cm (19 ½in)/2.8kg (6lb)
Lungs are ready for the world of air.

BIRTH.

Something To Think About …

Lanugo is the name of a fine downy hair that grows on the foetus. It helps to regulate temperature and disappears before birth. Some animals, such as elephants, are born still covered with it.

Chapter 05.0 **Environment & Society_**

05.1 Population Growth_

All around the world the growth of cities has followed the **mechanisation** of **agriculture** and **farming**. As the demand for workers to bring in the food decreased, people were forced to move to the cities to find work.

In the first instance, cities drew workers from farms to work in factories but as we have become more and more sophisticated in the way we produce things, the cities have become less and less important as **manufacturing** centres. In countries that are still developing, their major cities are still growing and still producing things. In countries which we describe as developed, the cities are full of **service industries** where nothing is actually made, but where it is sold or marketed.

As the populations in these **super-cities** grow, there are two choices in how to accommodate them: they can either build up or build out, or even both. Thus these massive **metropolises** swallow up the towns and villages on their periphery.

What most major cities have in common is how they gained their status. In almost all cases they will be near water, either on the coast, or a major river. Due to the ease of transport afforded by waterways (rivers, ports, coasts) it is vital to a city's growth to have access to water nearby.

Something To Think About ...

In England, the traditional way that a city is recognised is by the presence of a cathedral. Thus relatively small places can be cities, whilst some large settlements remain as towns.

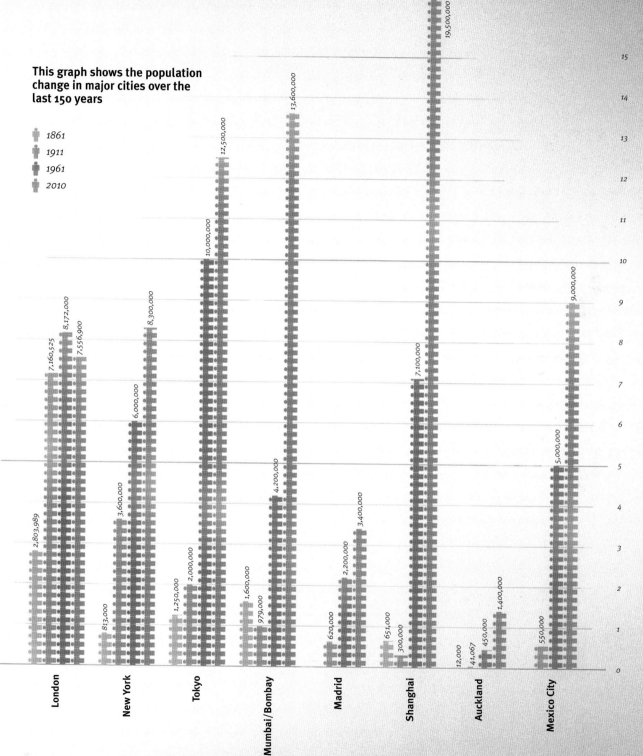

This graph shows the population change in major cities over the last 150 years

- 1861
- 1911
- 1961
- 2010

London
2,803,989
7,160,525
8,172,000
7,556,900

New York
813,000
3,600,000
6,000,000
8,300,000

Tokyo
1,250,000
2,000,000
10,000,000
12,500,000

Mumbai/Bombay
1,600,000
979,000
4,200,000
13,600,000

Madrid
620,000
2,200,000
3,400,000

Shanghai
651,000
300,000
7,100,000
19,500,000

Auckland
12,000
41,067
450,000
1,400,000

Mexico City
550,000
5,000,000
9,000,000

Total population in millions

0 1 2 3 4 5 6 7 8 9 10 11 12 13 14 15

05.2 Staple Food Production_

With a global population quickly approaching **seven billion** the big problem is how to feed everyone. Modern farming techniques have enabled us to grow larger quantities in increasingly smaller areas but it is always going to be a massive task. According to World Food Programme statistics almost one billion people do not have enough to eat. At the same time even optimistic figures suggest that globally 20% of food is wasted. It does not take much imagination to see that we could feed everyone.

In all societies certain foods are referred to as **staples**. These are generally cheap and readily available sources of nutrients and, especially in poorer countries, will make up a major part of the regular diet. Production of these staples is monopolised by a few countries around the globe. It is often cited that 80% of the world's food production is produced by only 20% of the world.

Something To Think About ...

Nearly 400,000,000 tonnes of rice are eaten each year around the world – equivalent to four trillion 100g (31/2 oz) portions.

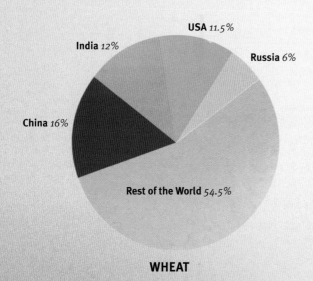

WHEAT

India *12%*
USA *11.5%*
Russia *6%*
China *16%*
Rest of the World *54.5%*

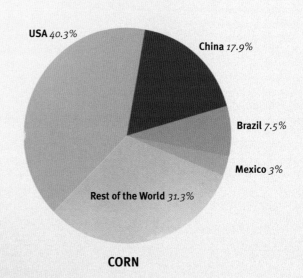

CORN

USA *40.3%*
China *17.9%*
Brazil *7.5%*
Mexico *3%*
Rest of the World *31.3%*

Production of staple foods by country of origin *(%)*

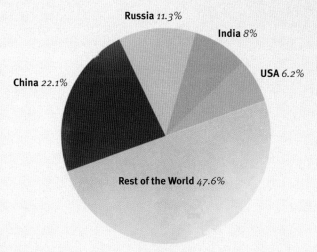

Russia *11.3%*

India *8%*

USA *6.2%*

China *22.1%*

Rest of the World *47.6%*

POTATOES

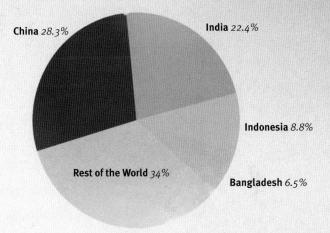

China *28.3%*

India *22.4%*

Indonesia *8.8%*

Rest of the World *34%*

Bangladesh *6.5%*

RICE

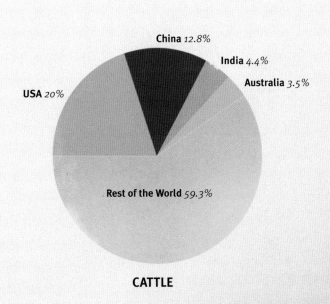

China *12.8%*

India *4.4%*

Australia *3.5%*

USA *20%*

Rest of the World *59.3%*

CATTLE

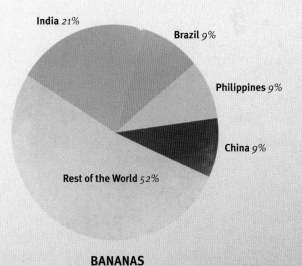

India *21%*

Brazil *9%*

Philippines *9%*

China *9%*

Rest of the World *52%*

BANANAS

05.3 The Science Of Art_

Art began roughly about 30,000 years ago with **cave drawings**. These depict what early modern man saw in his immediate environment, which is why animals occur predominantly.

In 1993 the British conceptual artist Damien Hirst exhibited *Mother and Child Divided*. The piece consists of four tanks of formaldehyde. Two of the tanks each contain half a cow, the other two each contain half a calf.

Art has travelled a *long* way but has never moved.

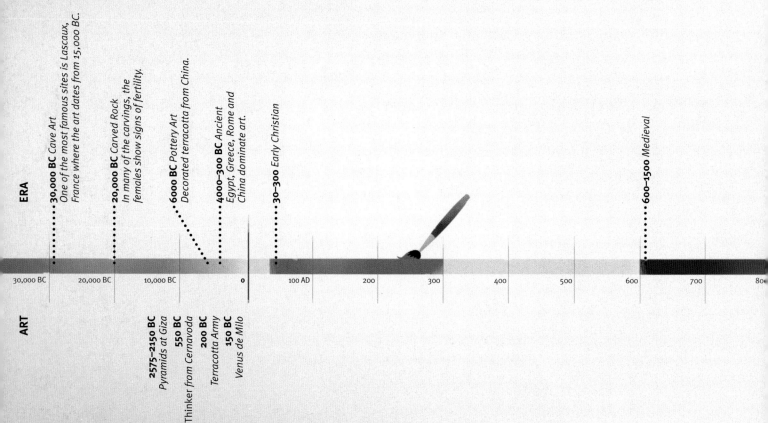

ERA

30,000 BC *Cave Art*
One of the most famous sites is Lascaux, France where the art dates from 15,000 BC.

20,000 BC *Carved Rock*
In many of the carvings, the females show signs of fertility.

6000 BC *Pottery Art*
Decorated terracotta from China.

4000–300 BC *Ancient*
Egypt, Greece, Rome and China dominate art.

30–300 Early Christian

600–1500 Medieval

30,000 BC   20,000 BC   10,000 BC   0   100 AD   200   300   400   500   600   700   800

ART

2575–2150 BC *Pyramids at Giza*
550 BC *Thinker from Cernavoda*
200 BC *Terracotta Army*
150 BC *Venus de Milo*

A timeline detailing some of art's greatest achievements and eras.

Something To Think About...

French artist Henri Matisse was a leading figure in modern art at the beginning of the 20th century. However, in 1961 one of his works, 'Le Bateau', was hung upside-down in the Museum of Modern Art, New York. None of many visitors to the museum ever noticed this mistake despite being a popular exhibit. It was finally hung the right way up after 47 days.

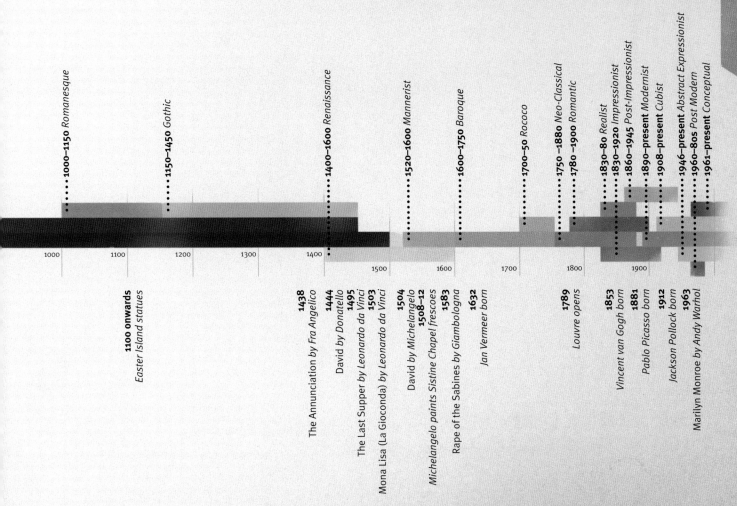

1000–1150 *Romanesque*

1150–1450 *Gothic*

1400–1600 *Renaissance*

1520–1600 *Mannerist*

1600–1750 *Baroque*

1700–50 *Rococo*

1750 –1880 *Neo-Classical*

1780 –1900 *Romantic*

1830–80 *Realist*

1830–1920 *Impressionist*

1860–1945 *Post-Impressionist*

1890–present *Modernist*

1908–present *Cubist*

1946–present *Abstract Expressionist*

1960–80s *Post Modern*

1961–present *Conceptual*

1000 1100 1200 1300 1400 1500 1600 1700 1800 1900

1100 onwards
Easter Island statues

1438
The Annunciation by Fra Angelico

1444
David by Donatello

1495
The Last Supper by Leonardo da Vinci

1503
Mona Lisa (La Gioconda) by Leonardo da Vinci

1504
David by Michelangelo

1508–12
Michelangelo paints Sistine Chapel frescoes

1583
Rape of the Sabines by Giambologna

1632
Jan Vermeer born

1789
Louvre opens

1853
Vincent van Gogh born

1881
Pablo Picasso born

1912
Jackson Pollock born

1963
Marilyn Monroe by Andy Warhol

The Sound Of Music_

From the banging of sticks on stretched animal skin right through to the banging of bones of rock, music – from the Greek phrase 'art for the muses' – has had a massive impact on human culture.

It is impossible to know how music first became such an important part of our lives but it is clear that nature provides ample example – from bird song through to the rhythmic chirping of insects.

A major movement of music is **Classical** and, as a whole, it covers a period of over 1,500 years. Whilst the development of styles over this period, up to the beginning of the 20th Century was relatively slow and restrained, since 1900 there have been many varied developments.

Thanks to the number of radio and television stations now available it is possible at any time of day or night to hear examples of all the musical genres seen on this page, going all the way back to the medieval period.

33,000 BC
A flute, made of hollowed-out bones, is one of the earliest musical instruments discovered. It is believed to be about 35,000 years old and was played by Neanderthals.

175 BC
The Mawangui Silk Texts. Written on silk, these Chinese philosophical works were found in a tomb in the city of Changsha, Hunan, China in 1973.

850
Historians uncover evidence of the earliest known mechanical instrument – a hydro-powered organ that played interchangeable cylinders automatically.

1764
Wolfgang Amadeus Mozart writes his first symphony at the age of eight.

1781
Mozart moves to Vienna and premières his masterpiece The Marriage of Figaro.

1809–present
The Brass Band style is popularised.

1877
Thomas Edison invents the phonograph on 12 August. He tests the machine using the nursery rhyme Mary had a Little Lamb.

1919
The theremin is invented by Russian professor Léon Theremin and is cited as one of the first electronic musical instruments, and the first ever that is played without being touched.

250 BC
Greek writings on music found.

500–1760
Early Classical period
This period can be divided into three subsets:
500–1400 Medieval
1400–1600 Renaissance
1600–1760 Baroque.

1750–1820
The music which was dominant during this time can be characterised by simple melodies and sonatas. Most composers used the piano to write their pieces.

1773
The Waltz becomes popular in Vienna.

1801
Beethoven performs his Symphony #1 in C Major for the first time in Vienna.

1860
The earliest recordings of a human's voice are recorded on a phonautograph by Edouard-Léon Scott de Martinville. But the sounds cannot be played back.

1890
Blues music develops, predominately in the Deep South of the USA.

1924
The first high-fidelity sound recording is made using equipment that minimised distortion and provided faithful sound

Something To Think About ...

In 2008, 95% of all music that was downloaded from the Internet was illegally sourced and it is estimated that on an average teenager's iPod 800 of the songs are pirated. In 2010, iTunes – the world's most popular online digital media store – announced that it had sold 10,000,000,000 song downloads in under seven years of operating.

A timeline of some of music's greatest achievements.

Magnetic tape is invented and revolutionises recording and broadcasting music.

1935
The first reel-to-reel tape recorder – known as K1 – is demonstrated using magnetic tape invented by German-Austrian engineer Fritz-Pfleumer.

1948
Record company Columbia introduces the first LP (Long Playing) record. It can play 17 minutes of music on each side.

1963
At age 13 'Little' Stevie Wonder has his first major hit Fingertips (Pt. 2), which was recorded when he was 12.

1966
Bob Goldstein coins the word 'multimedia'.

1977
Punk music changes the musical landscape.

1982
Michael Jackson releases Thriller. The album is still ranked as one of the bestselling albums of all time, due in part to the accompanying seven music videos of singles taken from the album.

1999
Shawn Fanning and Shaun Parker create Napster, the first file-sharing program for digital audio players.

2008
In November, for the first time, music downloads via the Internet outsell CDs. iTunes announces it has sold over a billion songs through their iTunes store.

1934
The Hammond electric organ is invented by American engineer Laurens Hammond.

1946
Elvis Aaron Presley is bought his first guitar from a Tupelo hardware store – it cost $12.95.

1951
Computer programmer Geoff Hill programmes a computer in Australia to perform a melody – the first demonstration of computer-generated music.

1964
Liverpool group The Beatles perform to 73 million viewers on US TV – The Ed Sullivan Show.

1976–1982
Manufacturers Phillips and Sony develop the first type of compact disc.

1981
MTV is launched. The first video shown is Video Killed the Radio Star by The Buggles.

1994
The Rolling Stones become the first band to perform live over Internet radio – a cyberspace multicast.

2001
Apple launches the sleek iPod – a portable media player – on 23 October.

2010
Teenage pop star Justin Bieber's videos are viewed over a billion times on website www.youtube.com.

Great Reads In Time_

The Bestselling Books of All Time.

Copies Sold (in millions)

The Dream of the Red Chamber (1791) Cao Xueqin
100 million copies sold
Xueqin only wrote the first 80
of its 120, chapters.

A Tale of Two Cities (1859) Charles Dickens
200 million copies sold
Issued as 31 weekly instalments in
Dickens' Magazine *All the Year Round.*

Heidi (1880) Johanna Spyri
60 million copies sold
Broadcast of a 1968 American Football League game
was ended early for a transmission of an adaptation
of *Heidi*. The last minute of the game saw an
amazing comeback by the Oakland Raiders
that no television viewer saw.

She (1887) H. Rider Haggard
65 million copies sold
'She' is short for 'she who
must be obeyed'.

Le Petit Prince (1943) Antoine de Saint-Exupéry
80 million copies sold
La Petit Prince (The Little Prince) is set on Asteroid
B612. A real asteroid discovered in 1993, 46610
Besixdouze was named as a tribute.

Something To Think About …

While the Bible has sold over four billion copies to date, J. K. Rowling's series of seven Harry Potter books is the bestselling series of books in modern times, selling over 450 million books since *Harry Potter and the Philosopher's Stone* in 1997, as well as a multi-billion dollar Hollywood film franchise.

The Lion, the Witch and the Wardrobe (1950) C. S. Lewis
85 million copies sold
The first in the series of seven books covering *The Chronicles of Narnia*. Lewis died on the day that John F. Kennedy was assassinated.

Catcher in the Rye (1951) J. D. Salinger
120 million copies sold
John Lennon's killer, Mark Chapman, was carrying a copy when he shot the rock star in 1980.

The Lord of the Rings (1955) J. R. R. Tolkien
150 million copies sold
The Lord of the Rings took 12 years to write and six more before it was published.

The Alchemist (1988) Paulo Coelho
65 million copies sold
The most translated novel by a living author. Coelho has a blog from where it is possible to download some of his novels for free.

The da Vinci Code (2003) Dan Brown
80 million copies sold
Although clearly a work of fiction, the book has created a campaign of 'da Vinci Code' denial amongst some Christian groups.

The Dawn of Television_

In the developed world almost every house has one, and many have more than one.
The television, invented in 1925 by Scotsman **John Logie Baird**, has taken over the world
in less than a century and has changed the way we live.

In the developed world the average person will watch over 20 hours of television per
week. Other than working and sleeping, it is the activity we spend most of our time doing.
When we are not watching television, we spend a lot of time talking about the
programmes we have seen.

Whilst viewing figures and **television ownership** were already high, the introduction of
satellite television and the expansion of the number of channels available, has given sales
of television sets a further boost. With so many options it is not uncommon for the members
of an average family to all be watching different programmes at the same time. In the USA,
for instance, over 75% of households have more than one set and over 50% have
three or more.

1900
Russian scientist Constantin Perskyi coins the word 'television'.

1906
Russian scientist Boris Rosing builds first mechanical television set incorporating the cathode ray tube.

2 October 1925
Scottish inventor John Logie Baird gives a first demonstration of moving images on a television set.

1928
American Charles Jenkins opens first television station.

30 March 1930
BBC begins test broadcasts.

1936
BBC begins broadcasts from Alexandra Palace. There are still fewer than 1,000 sets worldwide.

1936
First televised sports event – the Berlin Olympics.

1940
American Peter Goldmark (who works for the CBS network) invents colour television.

1939–45
Television transmission halted almost everywhere during the Second World War. By now, around 20,000 sets purchased in the UK.

1941
Bulova Watches are advertised – the first television commercial. Twenty seconds cost $9 (US).

1946
John Logie Baird dies.

5 October 1947
President Harry Truman broadcasts from the White House for the first time.

1949
1,000,000 television sets in the USA.

1951

30 June 1952
The Guiding Line premieres on US TV. It becomes the world's longest running soap opera. Ended in September 2009.

1953
25,000,000 television sets in the USA.

1954
Football World Cup televised.

1954
Colour introduced to sets in the USA.

1960
Coronation Street begins in the UK. It is the longest running soap still on air.

1962
Telstar – the first satellite to relay television is launched.

20 July 1969
The Moon Landing is watched by 600 million people.

6th September 1997
Two billion people watch Princess Diana's funeral.

2007
Bullfighting taken off state-run Spanish television.

2009
Televisions with 3D capability go on sale.

Something To Think About ...

In 1982 Seiko produced a Television Watch. The screen was 3.8cm (1.5 in).

129

The Introduction Of Cinema_

Many people consider the 1906 Australian film *The Story of the Kelly Gang* to be the first ever feature film. Running at 70 minutes it was much longer than anything that had come before and it hit the screens just over ten years after the French **Lumière Brothers invented cinema** as we know it.

Since Auguste and Louis Lumière held their first public screening in 1895 there have really only been **two major advances** in cinema. *Don Juan* was the first film to have **synchronised sound**, although it had no dialogue. The first 'real' talkie was *The Jazz Singer*, released a year later in 1927. Many film stars' careers ended with the introduction of sound but the industry as a whole never looked back.

The other major advance came with the **arrival of colour**. A two-colour system had been in use since the mid 1910s but full three-colour production did not arrive until 1932 with Disney's *Flowers and Trees*.

Since then there have been further advances mainly to do with the size and shape of the projected image. A big obsession has always been with **three-dimensional** (3D) screening. This technology has been around since the 1920s and had a first golden era in the 1950s after which it went into decline until the early part of the 21st Century when it has entered again into the mainstream. Many blockbusters are now produced in both 2D and 3D formats.

Something To Think About ...

The Academy Award of Merit is better known as an **Oscar**. The Academy of Motion Picture Arts and Sciences was formed in 1927.

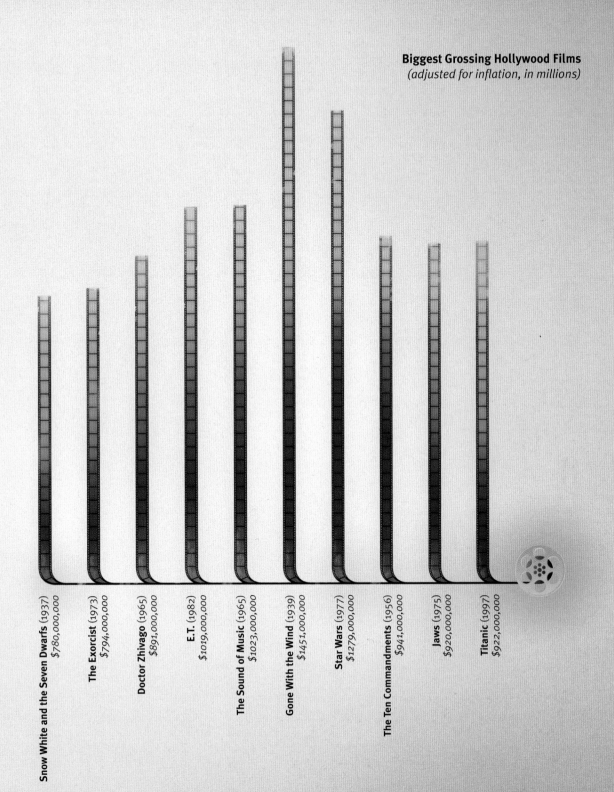

Biggest Grossing Hollywood Films
(adjusted for inflation, in millions)

Snow White and the Seven Dwarfs (1937)
$780,000,000

The Exorcist (1973)
$794,000,000

Doctor Zhivago (1965)
$891,000,000

E.T. (1982)
$1019,000,000

The Sound of Music (1965)
$1023,000,000

Gone With the Wind (1939)
$1451,000,000

Star Wars (1977)
$1279,000,000

The Ten Commandments (1956)
$941,000,000

Jaws (1975)
$920,000,000

Titanic (1997)
$922,000,000

Sport's Date With History_

A timeline of some of sport's greatest moments...

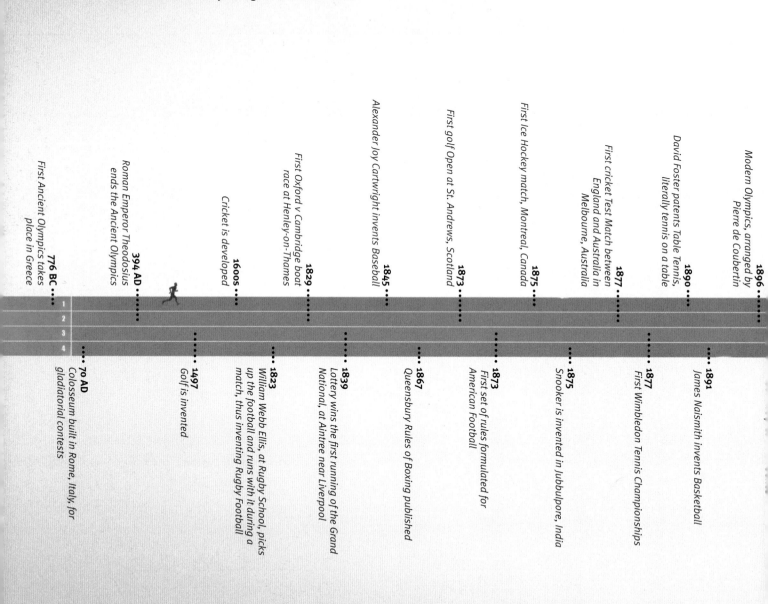

776 BC
First Ancient Olympics takes place in Greece

70 AD
Colosseum built in Rome, Italy, for gladiatorial contests

394 AD
Roman Emperor Theodosius ends the Ancient Olympics

1497
Golf is invented

1600s
Cricket is developed

1823
William Webb Ellis, at Rugby School, picks up the football and runs with it during a match, thus inventing Rugby Football

1829
First Oxford v Cambridge boat race at Henley-on-Thames

1839
Lottery wins the first running of the Grand National, at Aintree near Liverpool

1845
Alexander Joy Cartwright invents Baseball

1867
Queensbury Rules of Boxing published

1873
First golf Open at St. Andrews, Scotland

1873
First set of rules formulated for American Football

1875
First Ice Hockey match, Montreal, Canada

1875
Snooker is invented in Jubbulpore, India

1877
First cricket Test Match between England and Australia in Melbourne, Australia

1877
First Wimbledon Tennis Championships

1890
David Foster patents Table Tennis, literally tennis on a table

1891
James Naismith invents Basketball

1896
Modern Olympics, arranged by Pierre de Coubertin

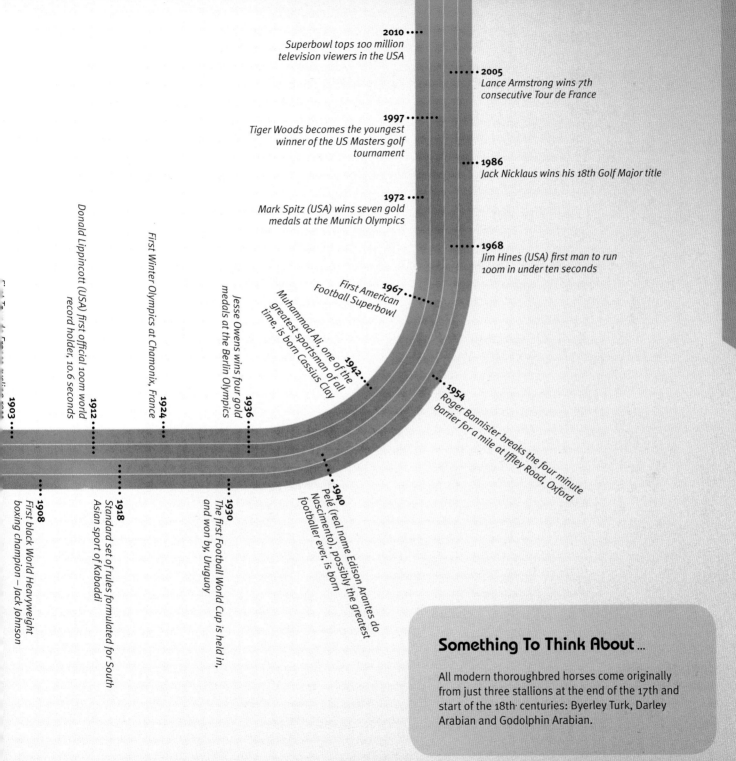

2010 • • • •
*Superbowl tops 100 million
television viewers in the USA*

2005
*Lance Armstrong wins 7th
consecutive Tour de France*

1997 • • • • • • •
*Tiger Woods becomes the youngest
winner of the US Masters golf
tournament*

1986
Jack Nicklaus wins his 18th Golf Major title

1972 • • • •
*Mark Spitz (USA) wins seven gold
medals at the Munich Olympics*

1968
*Jim Hines (USA) first man to run
100m in under ten seconds*

1967
*First American
Football Superbowl*

1954
*Roger Bannister breaks the four minute
barrier for a mile at Iffley Road, Oxford*

1942
*Muhammad Ali, one of the
greatest sportsman of all
time, is born Cassius Clay*

1940
*Pelé (real name Edison Arantes do
Nascimento), possibly the greatest
footballer ever, is born*

1936
*Jesse Owens wins four gold
medals at the Berlin Olympics*

1930
*The first Football World Cup is held in,
and won by, Uruguay*

1924
First Winter Olympics at Chamonix, France

1918
*Standard set of rules formulated for South
Asian sport of Kabaddi*

1912
*Donald Lippincott (USA) first official 100m world
record holder, 10.6 seconds*

1908
*First black World Heavyweight
boxing champion – Jack Johnson*

1903

Something To Think About...

All modern thoroughbred horses come originally
from just three stallions at the end of the 17th and
start of the 18th· centuries: Byerley Turk, Darley
Arabian and Godolphin Arabian.

133

Languages Of The World_

150,000 years ago humans started talking ... we haven't shut up since.

It is often said that America and England are two countries separated by a common language; the peoples of the Earth, however, are currently speaking nearly 7,000 languages.

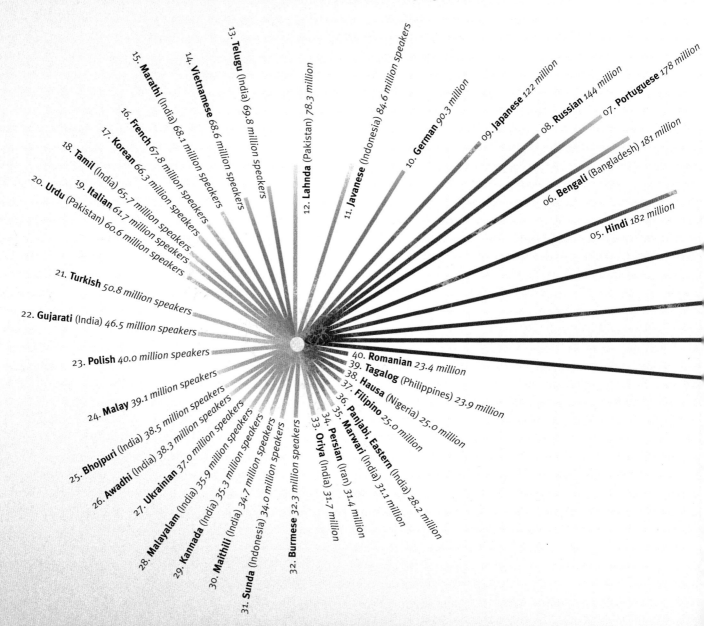

- 15. **Marathi** (India) 68.1 million speakers
- 14. **Vietnamese** 68.6 million speakers
- 13. **Telugu** (India) 69.8 million speakers
- 16. **French** 67.8 million speakers
- 17. **Korean** 66.3 million speakers
- 18. **Tamil** (India) 65.7 million speakers
- 19. **Italian** 61.7 million speakers
- 20. **Urdu** (Pakistan) 60.6 million speakers
- 21. **Turkish** 50.8 million speakers
- 22. **Gujarati** (India) 46.5 million speakers
- 23. **Polish** 40.0 million speakers
- 24. **Malay** 39.1 million speakers
- 25. **Bhojpuri** (India) 38.5 million speakers
- 26. **Awadhi** (India) 38.3 million speakers
- 27. **Ukrainian** 37.0 million speakers
- 28. **Malayalam** (India) 35.9 million speakers
- 29. **Kannada** (India) 35.3 million speakers
- 30. **Maithili** (India) 34.7 million speakers
- 31. **Sunda** (Indonesia) 34.0 million speakers
- 32. **Burmese** 32.3 million speakers
- 33. **Oriya** (India) 31.7 million
- 34. **Marwari** (India) 31.1 million
- 35. **Panjabi, Eastern** (India) 28.2 million
- 36. **Persian** (Iran) 31.4 million
- 37. **Filipino** 25.0 million
- 38. **Hausa** (Nigeria) 25.0 million
- 39. **Tagalog** (Philippines) 23.9 million
- 40. **Romanian** 23.4 million
- 12. **Lahnda** (Pakistan) 78.3 million
- 11. **Javanese** (Indonesia) 84.6 million speakers
- 10. **German** 90.3 million
- 09. **Japanese** 122 million
- 08. **Russian** 144 million
- 07. **Portuguese** 178 million
- 06. **Bengali** (Bangladesh) 181 million
- 05. **Hindi** 182 million

Something To Think About ...

Of the almost 7,000 languages in the world, more than half are expected to die out within the next 100 years. This trend was illustrated by the death of Marie Smith Jones in Anchorage, Alaska, in 2008 at the age of 89. She is believed to have been the last native speaker of the Eyak language, once spoken in southern Alaska near the mouth of the Copper River. In her later years she helped researchers at the University of Alaska compile an Eyak dictionary, so that it would have a chance of being revived in the future.

. **Arabic** 221 million

03. **English** 328 million

02. **Spanish** 329 million

01. **Chinese** (including Mandarin, Gan, Hakka, Huizhou, Jinyu, Min Bei, Min Dong, Min Nan, Min Zhong, Xiang, Wu, Yue) 1,213 million

In many cases, the number of people who speak a country's language is almost equal to its population. This is because not many people outside of that country have it as a first language. Of all the languages, English and Spanish are the two that have most outstripped their native populations.

Pollution And The Planet_

In a recent list of the **world's top ten most polluted cities** seven of them had gained their notoriety due to an increased dependency on **driving cars**. Part of the problem is that many people cannot afford to live in the city where they work and so they have to drive in to get to their job. This is *the* major concern in cities such as **Beijing**, **Cairo**, **Dhaka** and **New Delhi** and most especially in **Buenos Aires** where the **population increases** four-fold during the daytime.

Tanzania's capital **Dar Es Salaam** contains 80% of the country's industry and the residents burn **waste and biomass** on the streets. **Moscow's** recent **forest fires** have added to its pollution, whilst **Mexico City** has a combination of industry and cars compounded by dry, hot spells that add to this pollution.

The last two cities in the hall of shame are **Dzerzhinsk** in Russia and China's **Linfen**. Dzerzhinsk is where the Soviet Union produced many of its biological and chemical weapons during the Cold War up until the 1990s. This 'secret' city is still suffering from the poor management of this **industrial output**. Linfen, officially the most polluted city in the world, has the simple combination of cars, high population and **coal-fired power stations** to blame.

The Earth's Top Six Most Harmful Pollutants

	Caused by	Major problem
1. Carbon Dioxide	*Burning fossil fuels and deforestation*	*Increases global warming*
2. Nitrogen Dioxide	*Burning fossil fuels*	*Attacks the Earth's protective ozone layer*
3. Particulate Matter	*Roads, fires, construction*	*Gets into the lungs*
4. Sulphur Dioxide and Chlorofluorocarbons	*Burning fossil fuels*	*Constricts tubes in the lungs*
5. Lead	*Industry (used to be in petrol)*	*Affects the nervous system, kidney function, immune system amongst others*
6. Carbon Monoxide	*Mainly from automobile exhausts*	*Reduces oxygen intake*

Rest of the world *32.93%*

Something To Think About ...

In December 1952 there was a build-up of smog in London. It is estimated that 4,000 people died as a direct result of this polluted air. It led to the 1956 Clean Air Act.

The world's top ten worst polluters
In global percentage and annual CO_2 emissions (in thousands of tonnes)

6. **Germany** *2.69%*
(787,936)

7. **Canada** *1.90%*
(557,340)

8. **United Kingdom** *1.84%*
(539,617)

5. **Japan** *4.28%*
(1,254,543)

9. **South Korea** *1.72%*
(503,321)

4. **Russia** *5.24%*
(1,537,357)

10. **Iran** *1.69%*
(495,987)

3. **India** *5.50%*
(1,612,362)

1. **China** *22.30%*
(29,321,302)

2. **United States** *19.91%*
(6,538,367)

Our Changing World: Global Warming_

The term 'global warming' was first coined in 1975 by Wallace Broecker in an article he wrote for *Science* titled: *Climatic Change: Are We on the Brink of a Pronounced Global Warming?*. **Climate change** and the effect it may have on the planet is one of the most pressing problems facing governments around the world but this has not led to any decisive action.

The problem is that whilst the evidence shows that the **average global temperature has risen** by 1.4° Fahrenheit (0.8° Centigrade) since accurate records began in 1880, there is no real consensus on what the future consequences of further warming, or even what the future change, might be. This lack of agreement has meant that no clear strategy or desire for action to contain it has been reached by the world's most powerful industrial nations.

Scientists with a pessimistic view of our future predict that the speed of the rise in temperature is increasing and may soon reach a point beyond which we are unable to turn back the damage to the world's atmospheres, oceans and **ecosystems is unrepairable**. The optimists regard the Earth, however, as a **self-regulating entity** and believe that this current increase in temperature is no more than a blip that will turn the other way before long. The Earth's meteorological history is full of these blips.

If the pessimists are to be believed and the increase continues, the effect on the planet could be catastrophic. For instance, with rainfall increasing, flooding would occur which would lead to an erosion of viable farming areas and thus, ultimately, a world food shortage. The level of the sea is also increased by the warming and the water from the **melting ice caps**.

Something To Think About ...

One of the major stated causes of global warming is CO2 emission. Cars, trains and aeroplanes would top most people's list of the worst offenders but not according to a 2008 UN Report which found that livestock were the cause of 18% of global emissions. The methane from their wind and poo contributes in a large way to this figure as it is 20 times more damaging than carbon dioxide.

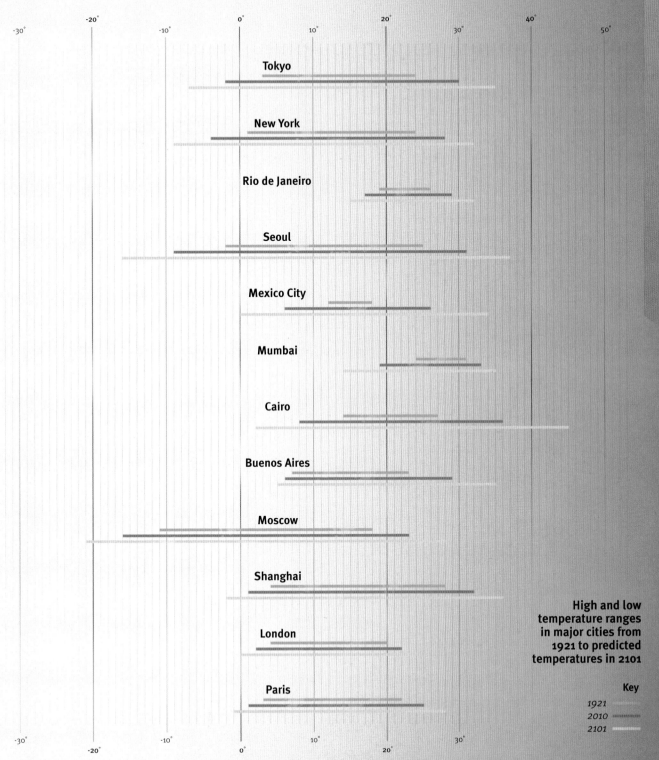

High and low temperature ranges in major cities from 1921 to predicted temperatures in 2101

Key

1921

2010

2101

Seven Man-made Wonders Of The World_

Everything that you see around you is made from material that has always been here. When you think about that fact it makes **Man's achievements** even more astonishing. Apollo 11, the first craft to leave our atmosphere and successfully land on another planet was built using raw materials that were, in effect, available to the caveman.

The Moon landing is no less incredible than the **Pyramids**. That they have lasted nearly 5,000 years and are the only remaining item from the mythical Ancient Wonders of the World is testament to their creators. And between these two events Man has continually surpassed previous generations, leaving a legacy at which we can only marvel.

The Seven Man Made Wonders of the World shown here are in no particular order.

The Great Pyramids
Built around 2560 BC
Giza, Egypt

Series of pyramids built for the 4th Dynasty pharaoh Khufu. Notable for the astronomical link-up with Orion's Belt.

Taj Mahal
Finished 1653
Agra, India

A mausoleum built by Shah Jaham in memory of his wife Mumtaz Mahal. Considered by many as one of the most beautiful man-made buildings in the world, and a globally recognised symbol of eternal love.

Machu Picchu
1400s
Urubamba Valley, Peru

The Lost City of the Incas, as it is commonly referred to, had gone undiscovered by the rest of the world until 1911 and, even today, remains relatively intact.

Apollo 11
Landed on Moon, July 20, 1969
The Moon

The first craft – made by materials found on Earth – that travelled about 384,393km (238,857 miles)to another celestial body. It returned home safely and marked a significant moment in human technological history.

Mount Rushmore
1941
Keystone, South Dakota, USA

The heads of four important US Presidents – George Washington, Thomas Jefferson, Theodore Roosevelt and Abraham Lincoln – carved into the granite rock of the Black Hills region of South Dakota. Each head is about 18m (60ft) high and were created as an attempt to improve tourism in the area. It worked.

Great Wall of China
5thC BC–16thC[b]
China

This ancient wall meanders around Northern China at about 8,851km (5,500 miles) in length and was built to defend the borders against nomadic invaders.

Stonehenge
c. 2700 BC
Wiltshire, United Kingdom

No one is exactly sure who made Stonehenge. Or how.

Chapter 06.0 **Making History_**

The Spread Of Man Across The Globe_

A combination of **genetic study** (of Mitochondrial DNA) and the discovery of **early human fossils** has allowed modern scientists to track humans' first migration patterns out of Africa – the continent many believe was the birthplace of human life. Out of Africa, the spread of early man across the globe was one of our most important evolutionary journeys and the first steps to creating civilisation and settlements.

45–52 tya
A mini-ice age occurs causing further movement of Homo Sapiens *into Europe – up the Danube to Hungary and Austria.*

52–65 tya
The planet warms and groupings of Homo Sapiens *start heading north to the Levant and into Europe.*

90–115 tya
The Levant group die out due to a global freeze.

8–10 tya
Final collapse of the last Ice Age. Sahara desert region is characterised as a sloping grassland.

115–135 tya
Some groups make it as as the Levant – the join point between western A the eastern Mediterranea north-east Africa– throug open Northern Gate.

135–160 tya
Four large groupings of Homo Sapiens *travel to Cape of Good Hope, Congo Basin, Ivory Coast and Herto, Ethiopia.*

160 tya
Homo sapiens *origi in East Africa and di into groupings.*

Something To Think About ...

While modern *Homo sapiens* has a desire to travel the globe for entertainment, the early spread of humanity across the planet was motivated primarily by the search for food and warmer climates. Nomadic tribes followed the migration patterns of the herd animals they hunted. Our *Homo sapiens*' ability to adapt and thrive in new and harsh conditions gave early humans a key advantage over *Homo erectus* and aided his global domination.

25–40 tya
Central Asian groups move towards Europe, north into the Arctic Circle and join east Asians in the spread into north-east Eurasia.

22–25 tya
What will become Native Americans cross the Bering Land Bridge connecting Siberia and Alaska.

19–22 tya
The last Ice Age occurs. North American groups depopulate. Some groups survive.

40–45 tya
Groups of Homo sapiens from east Asian coast move west to Central Asia, from Pakistan to central Asia, and from Indo-China to the Qing-Hai Plateau.

15–19 tya
The Last Glacial Maximum (LGM) – a period when huge areas of land are covered in ice sheets – occurs. In North America, south of the ice, groups of Homo sapiens continue to develop and diversify.

10–12.5 tya
North America is repopulated.

75–85 tya
From Sri Lanka they continue round the coast all the way to South China.

85–90 tya
A grouping of Homo sapiens cross the mouth of the Red Sea and heads along the coast to India – all non-African humans are descended from this group.

12.5–15 tya
Coastal routes open around South America.

74 tya
Mt Toba (in Sumatra, western Indonesia) erupts creating a nuclear winter and a 1,000 year-long ice age. World population drops below 10,000, and possibly as low as 1,000 couples.

65–74 tya
The surviving groups spread into Australia and New Guinea away from the intense cold of the Lower Pleniglacial.

[tya – thousand years ago]   **Homo sapiens**   Neanderthals   Early hominids

The End Of Nomadic Man_

From the very earliest days of our evolution, man was a **hunter-gatherer** roaming from coast to coast following the source of food and making camp wherever safe until all the nearby food ran out or had moved on. Then, about **10,000 years ago,** the nomadic lifestyle came to an end and early settlements were formed.

The catalyst for this **Neolithic Revolution** was the end of the last Ice Age. As temperatures rose again, the supply of **animals and vegetation increased** and the need to move around as often decreased. Some groups found that they could remain in the same place for longer periods, and once they had survived a year in the same location, all the problems relating to that site through each of the seasons had been shown to be surmountable.

This period coincided with the realisation that some animals were prepared to stay near human settlements when provided with feed. As long as they were provided nourishment, the animals would not move on and **subsistence farming** was created. It didn't necessarily work everywhere it was tried, but when it didn't the people just moved on and tried somewhere else.

Factors that were likely to increase the likelihood of early settlements were the **availability of fresh water** and the **abundance of edible flora.**

Something To Think About...

One of the first results of the change from hunter-gathering to early settler was a rise in disease due to an increased lack of variation in the diet. However, settling did result in a growth in population as, suddenly, it was easier to look after infants when not constantly on the move.

Changes in diet from early man to the present day.

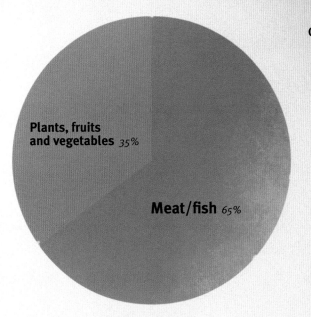

Plants, fruits and vegetables *35%*

Meat/fish *65%*

Hunter-gatherer
High in protein, low in carbohydrates

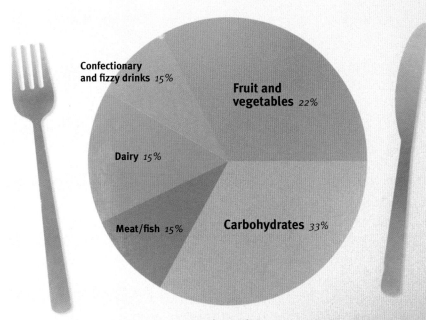

Confectionary and fizzy drinks *15%*

Fruit and vegetables *22%*

Dairy *15%*

Meat/fish *15%*

Carbohydrates *33%*

Modern Diet
Low in protein, high in carbohydrates

The Empires_

They came, they saw, they conquered.

Throughout history powerful countries have made the decision to spread their control beyond their own borders. This empire building, by its nature, generally requires the use of force – be it **military or political**. King Sargon the Great built the first empire around the city of Akkad (Iraq) in 2300 BC. The last empire in the truest sense of the term was the USSR (Union of Soviet Socialist Republics) that finally broke up in the early 1990s. The importance of these empires is that they **exported their culture**, beliefs and language to the territories they conquered. In some cases these influences held – the Spanish culture in Argentina is a perfect example.

Roman Empire ······
27 BC–474 AD

Capital:
Rome
Coverage at maximum extent:
North to Scotland, south to Sudan, west to Portugal and Morocco, east to Iraq and Azerbaijan.
Main contribution to their colonies:
Modern language

*200 BC   100 BC   **year 0**   100 AD*

Egyptian Empire ·····
16th–11th Century BC

Capital:
Thebes, in the main but also at different times Akhetaten and Pi-Ramesses
Coverage at maximum extent:
North and east to Syria, South to Sudan, West to Libya.
Main contribution to their colonies:
The Pyramids

Ancient Greece ·····
5th–4th Century BC

Capital:
Athens
Coverage at maximum extent:
North to Ukraine, south to Libya, west to Spain, east to the east coast of the Black Sea.
Main contribution to their colonies:
Philosophy

Chinese Empire
221 BC–1911 AD

Capital:
Various but mainly Beijing
Coverage at maximum extent:
Mainly within the borders of what we now call China.
Main contribution to their colonies:
Bureaucracy

Spanish Empire
1521–1643

Capital:
Madrid
Coverage at maximum extent:
*Mainly to the west encompassing North America,
South America (apart from Brazil), Philippines to the east,
Small pockets of Africa and India.*
Main contribution to their colonies:
Roman Catholicism

Mongol Empire
1206–1368

Capital:
Zhongdu (now called Beijing)
Coverage at maximum extent:
*The largest contiguous Empire; north to Russia, south to
Korea and Pakistan, west to Poland, east to China.*
Main contribution to their colonies:
Organised warfare

British Empire
Late 16th C–mid-20th C

Capital:
London
Coverage at maximum extent:
*West to Canada and eastern America, south to South Africa,
east to New Zealand and Australia. India.*
Main contribution to their colonies:
Constitutional government

History Of Modern Warfare_

The first recorded war in history was between Sumer (now in Iraq) and Elam (Iran) and occurred around 2700 BC. Since this date, there has not been a day when there has not been a war taking place somewhere on Earth.

The spoils of war may well usually be **material possessions** but war is also heavily dictated by philosophical disputes over the aggressor's disapproval of the **way of life** of the opposition and a strong desire to impose its own set of values.

Whilst there has always been war, it was due to improved communication and transportation that the world was able to have a **full-scale conflict** that involved almost every continent. The First World War began in the summer of 1914 and concluded in late 1918. Just 21 years later another global conflict began in 1939 and lasted until 1945. This Second World War was only finally ended by the USA's use of the atomic bomb, and at the time there was a feeling that with this threat hanging over the planet, the days of global conflicts were over. Sadly this proved to be a false hope.

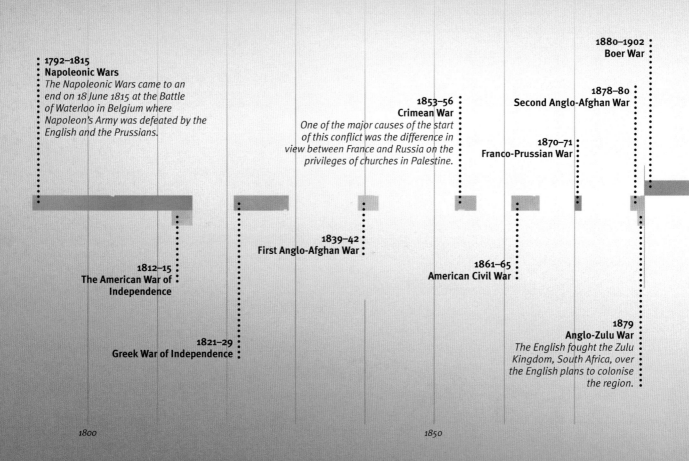

1880–1902
Boer War

1792–1815
Napoleonic Wars
The Napoleonic Wars came to an end on 18 June 1815 at the Battle of Waterloo in Belgium where Napoleon's Army was defeated by the English and the Prussians.

1853–56
Crimean War
One of the major causes of the start of this conflict was the difference in view between France and Russia on the privileges of churches in Palestine.

1878–80
Second Anglo-Afghan War

1870–71
Franco-Prussian War

1812–15
The American War of Independence

1839–42
First Anglo-Afghan War

1861–65
American Civil War

1821–29
Greek War of Independence

1879
Anglo-Zulu War
The English fought the Zulu Kingdom, South Africa, over the English plans to colonise the region.

1800

1850

Something To Think About...

Mutually Assured Destruction, generally abbreviated as MAD, is the theory by which peace is maintained due to the knowledge that if either side attacks the other, both sides will be annihilated.

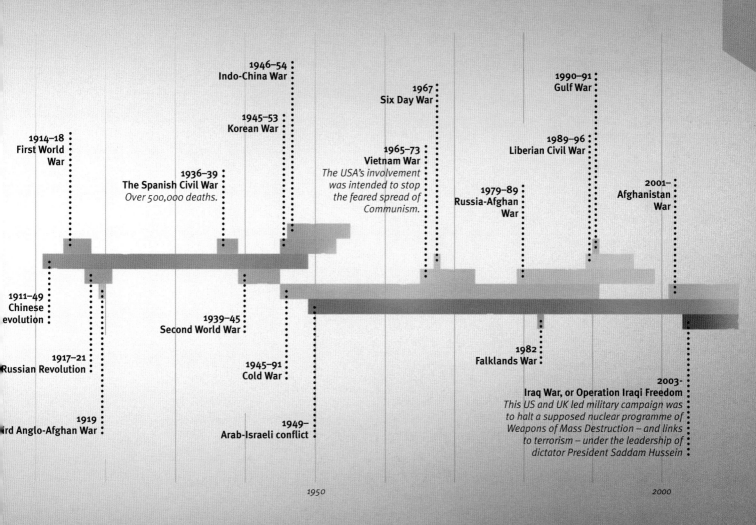

1946–54
Indo-China War

1967
Six Day War

1990–91
Gulf War

1945–53
Korean War

1914–18
First World War

1965–73
Vietnam War
The USA's involvement was intended to stop the feared spread of Communism.

1989–96
Liberian Civil War

1936–39
The Spanish Civil War
Over 500,000 deaths.

2001–
Afghanistan War

1979–89
Russia-Afghan War

1911–49
Chinese Revolution

1939–45
Second World War

1917–21
Russian Revolution

1945–91
Cold War

1982
Falklands War

1919
3rd Anglo-Afghan War

1949–
Arab-Israeli conflict

2003–
Iraq War, or Operation Iraqi Freedom
This US and UK led military campaign was to halt a supposed nuclear programme of Weapons of Mass Destruction – and links to terrorism – under the leadership of dictator President Saddam Hussein

The Five Years Of The First World War_

On the 28 June 1914 Gavrilo Princip, a Bosnian-Serb, shot dead **Archduke Franz Ferdinand**, the heir to the Habsburg empire. This event is always cited as the primary cause of the war, however, in effect, it was the straw that broke the back of a **delicate balance of alliances and treaties**. It led, like the toppling of one domino onto another, to the **collapse of world peace** and a conflict that lasted for five years.

At the centre of the conflict was Germany, concerned by the powers on either side, **France and Russia**, and jealous of **Britain's dominance of the seas**. France harboured a long-term hostility towards Germany dating back to the **Franco-Prussian War**. Meanwhile, Russia and the Austria-Hungarian Empire were both trying to **gain supremacy** in the Balkans.

The Archduke's death led to a declaration of war on Serbia by Austria. Germany, having promised support for Austria-Hungary, declared war on Russia, then France. The German invasion of Belgium triggered the terms of the **1839 Treaty of London** meaning Britain was obliged to declare war on Germany. Only five weeks after Princip pulled the trigger, the **world was at war**. Five years to the day after that shot was fired the war was finally concluded with the signing of the **Treaty of Versailles**.

28 June 1914
Assassination of Archduke Franz Ferdinand, heir to the empire of Habsburg.

28 July 1914
Austria declares war on Serbia.

1 August 1914
Germany declares war on Russia.

3 August 1914
Germany declares war on France, then invades Belgium.

4 August 1914
Britain declares war on Germany.

29 October 1914
Turkey joins forces with the Germans, forming the **Central Powers** – one of the two sides that fought in the war. The opposing side was the **Allied Powers** formed of England, France and the Russian Empire.

23 May 1915
Italy declares war on Germany and Austria.

Something To Think About ...

Nearly 10 million soldiers died and 21 million were wounded during the First World War. A total of 65 million soldiers were mobilised, equivalent to the current population of the UK.

6 April 1917
USA declares war on Germany.

5 December 1917
Armistice between Germany and Russia.

3 March 1918
Germany and Russia sign Treaty of Brest-Litovsk, marking Russia's exit from the war.

30 October 1918
Turkey makes peace with the Allied Powers.

3 November 1918
Austria makes peace with the Allied Powers

11 November 1918
Germany signs the Armistice. The end of the First World War is announced.

28 June 1919
The Treaty of Versailles is signed by Germany and the Allied Powers.

153

The Second World War _

The First World War was often referred to as 'the war to end war all wars'. This proved to be far from true and just 20 years after the signing of the **Treaty of Versailles** Germany's invasion of Poland forced Britain into declaring war.

Many things led indirectly to this breaking point but much of the blame for the eventual conflict has been placed at the door of Versailles. By imposing economical and social conditions upon Germany, which at the time seemed fair (but have since been re-evaluated as harsh), the seeds were sown for a second war. The resentment Germany's people and politicians felt towards these punishments, combined with the difficulty the country had in repairing its **economy after the First World War**, created a fertile ground for the rise of the National Socialists and **Hitler's Nazi party**.

The Second World War began on **3 September 1939** when Britain and France declared war on Germany two days after the German army invaded Poland. It was not until Japan, and then Germany, declared war on America in December 1941 that the USA joined the Allied Forces.

Germany surrendered on 7 May 1945. Japan followed on 14 August after Hiroshima and Nagasaki had been **annihilated by atomic bombs** dropped by the US Army.

In all, **50,000,000 people died** during the conflict. Only 30% of these were soldiers. Russia suffered the biggest losses (20,000,000 dead), whilst the Nazi's Final Solution saw the murder of 6,000,000 Jews.

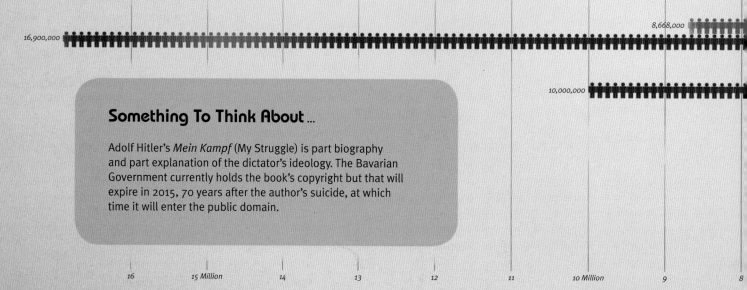

16,900,000

8,668,000

10,000,000

Something To Think About ...

Adolf Hitler's *Mein Kampf* (My Struggle) is part biography and part explanation of the dictator's ideology. The Bavarian Government currently holds the book's copyright but that will expire in 2015, 70 years after the author's suicide, at which time it will enter the public domain.

16   15 Million   14   13   12   11   10 Million   9   8

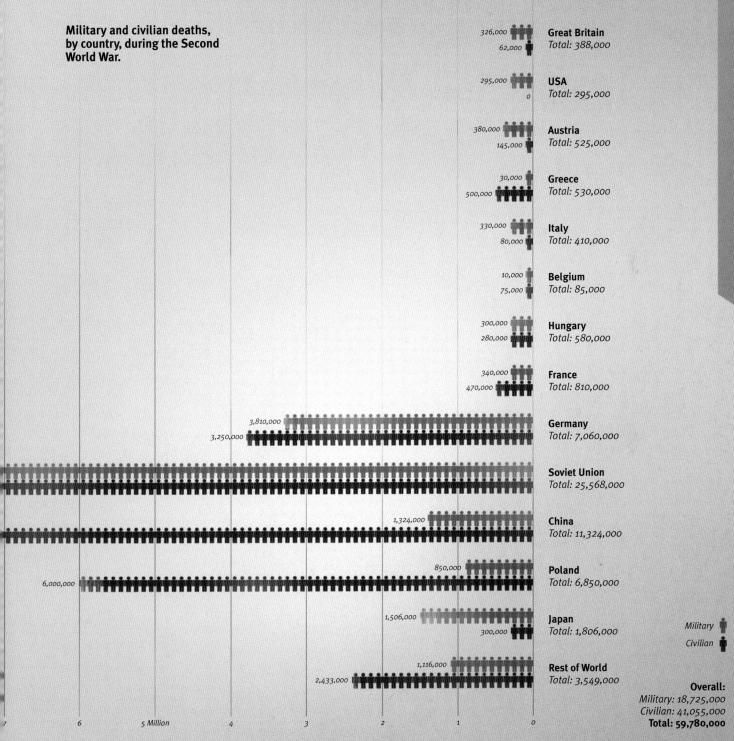

Military and civilian deaths, by country, during the Second World War.

Great Britain
Total: 388,000
326,000
62,000

USA
Total: 295,000
295,000
0

Austria
Total: 525,000
380,000
145,000

Greece
Total: 530,000
30,000
500,000

Italy
Total: 410,000
330,000
80,000

Belgium
Total: 85,000
10,000
75,000

Hungary
Total: 580,000
300,000
280,000

France
Total: 810,000
340,000
470,000

Germany
Total: 7,060,000
3,810,000
3,250,000

Soviet Union
Total: 25,568,000

China
Total: 11,324,000
1,324,000

Poland
Total: 6,850,000
850,000
6,000,000

Japan
Total: 1,806,000
1,506,000
300,000

Rest of World
Total: 3,549,000
1,116,000
2,433,000

Military
Civilian

7   6   5 Million   4   3   2   1   0

Overall:
Military: 18,725,000
Civilian: 41,055,000
Total: 59,780,000

Powerful Leaders Of The Past 2,000 Years_

Winston Churchill said that 'history is written by the victors' but this does not stop some of the defeated from entering the ranks of the **history makers**. If evil things happen because good people do nothing then it is fair to say that some of our most famous figures would not have come to the fore without the catalyst of the evil they fought.

Churchill himself is a good example of this. Whilst he was prominent in British politics before the Second World War he would not be the iconic figure he became without the 'help' of German Dictator Adolf Hitler.

Throughout history there have been 'good' men and 'evil' men. Whichever side of the **moral compass** they stood they all had one thing in common; the ability to make others follow them. This capacity may have stemmed from charisma, or intellect, or it may have been fear that made their followers fall into line.

Queen Victoria

Born/Died: *1819–1901*
In power: *1837–1901*
Role: *Queen of Great Britain and The Ruler of the British Empire*
Followers: *400, 000, 000*
Highlight: *Overseeing Britain's age of Industrial revolution, global economic progress and expansion of the Empire. Queen Victoria was also the first monarch to use the train.*

Mohandas Ghandi

Born/Died: *1869–1948*
In power: *1915–1948*
Role: *Politician and Father of India*
Followers: *310, 000, 000*
Highlight: *Ghandi's philosophies helped India gain independence from the British and inspired his millions of followers in the power of non-violent civil disobedience.*

Jesus Christ

Born/Died: *0BC–35 AD*
In power: *30 AD–Present*
Role: *Catalyst for foundation of Christianity*
Followers: *2,000,000,000*
Highlight: *Being the son of God, sacrificing himself for humanity, the resurrection and creating Christianity*

Genghis Khan

Born/Died: *1162–1227*
In power: *1206–1227*
Role: *Founder of Mongul Empire*
Followers: *100, 000, 000*
Highlight: *Born in Mongolia, Khan is often cited for his great military prowess and expanding his empire over almost all of Asia by the time of his death.*

Adolf Hitler

Born/Died: *1889–1945*
In power: *1933–1945*
Role: *Chancellor and Fuhrer of Germany*
Followers: *90, 000, 000*
Overview: *Ruled Germany for 12 years as a leader for poor Germans after WWI, led the Nazi party and authorised the annihilation of 6 million Jews via the Holocaust*

Julius Caesar

Born/Died: *100 BC–44 BC*
In power: *48 BC–44 BC*
Role: *Roman Dictator*
Followers: *55, 000, 000*
Highlight: *A highly respected Roman General and military strategist, credited with developing the expansion of Roman civilisation around Europe.*

Attila the Hun

Born/Died: *406–453*
In power: *433–453*
Role: *Ruler of the Hun Empire*
Followers: *Unknown*
Highlight: *Often referred to as the Scourge of God, Atilla was a powerful military strategist who killed his own brother so that he did not have to share ruling the empire. The cause of his death is unknown.*

Martin Luther King Jr

Born/Died: *1929–1968*
In power: *1957–1968*
Role: *Prominent leader in the African-American Civil Rights Movement*
Followers: *Unknown*
Highlight: *His 'I Have A Dream' speech in 1963 led to him becoming the youngest male recipient of the Nobel Peace Prize in 1964. He was assassinated in 1968.*

Winston Churchill

Born/Died: *1874–1965*
In power: *1940–45, 1951–55*
Role: *Prime Minister of Great Britain*
Followers: *46, 000, 000*
Highlight: *Leading the British, along with help from the rest of the Allies, to victory against the Nazi-led German Army in World War II. He was also elected twice as Prime Minister.*

The Rise Of The Superpowers_

A superpower is described as a nation that has the ability to **influence global events** and the **behaviour of less significant nations**. For a long period after the Second World War there were only two nations that fell into this category, the Soviet Union (USSR) and the USA. For nearly 40 years they held the balance of world power between them and the Cold War in which they were involved threatened the future of the planet.

With the collapse of communism, between 1989 and 1991, and the subsequent destruction of the USSR, the **power balance** of the world **shifted and fragmented** to such an extent that **the number of superpowers has risen**. What makes a superpower can subtly shift on an almost daily basis but it is generally accepted that there are currently five.

The USA has held its place at the top table and Russia has taken the still slightly warm seat once held by the USSR. Joining these two are China, with 20% of the world's population, India with over 17%, and the European Union with over a quarter of the world's Gross Domestic Product or GDP.

With a burgeoning economy Brazil is pushing for a place as a superpower, as is Japan, and within the next decade or so the number of superpowers in the world could increase to ten. At that stage a new term will perhaps need to be coined.

The USA's total military expenditure in 2009 was around seven times more than that of China.

USA
Population: *307,000,000*
Gross Domestic Product: *$14,000,000,000,000*
Nuclear weapons capability: *Yes*
Military expenditure (in 2009): *$663,255,000,000*
Tourist visits (per year): *54,900,000*

Something To Think About ...

The European Union (EU) is counted as a single entity because of the agreement between the member nations that holds them together. This includes; a single currency, the Euro (although not every member uses it) and a European Parliament, which has power over all the members.

European Union
Population: *500,000,000*
Gross Domestic Product : *$16,000,000,000,000*
Nuclear weapons capability: *Yes*
Military expenditure (in 2009):
France: $67,316,000,000 / UK: $69,271,000,000
Tourist visits (per year): *France 74,200,000*

Russia
Population: *142,000,000*
Gross Domestic Product: *$1,300,000,000,000*
Nuclear weapons capability: *Yes*
Military expenditure (in 2009): *$61,000,000,000*
Tourist visits (per year): *20,600,000 (2007)*

France is the most popular tourist destination in the world.

China
Population: *1,325,000,000*
Gross Domestic Product: *$5,000,000,000,000*
Nuclear weapons capability: *Yes*
Military expenditure (in 2009): *$98,800,000,000*
Tourist visits (per year): *50,900,000*

India
Population: *1,140,000,000*
Gross Domestic Product: *$1,250,000,000,000*
Nuclear weapons capability: *Yes*
Military expenditure (in 2009): *$36,600,000,000*
Tourist visits (per year): *5,000,000*

159

The Fall Of Communism_

Like two playing cards balanced against one another, the USA and the Soviet Union dictated the security of the world for 40 years after the end of the Second World War. Like playing cards themselves, this was a delicate balance and the house of cards could have toppled at any moment. When the Soviet Union and the communist bloc disintegrated at the end of the 1980s the world changed forever.

The house of cards analogy has probably never been more apt than when used to describe the **collapse of communism**. During the 1980s, the communist government in Poland faced major anti-communist opposition and when the **trade unions won in the elections**, the first card fell. Developments in global communication meant it was possible to broadcast this news in spite of state ownership of domestic media channels, and it was only two months before Hungary went the same way.

Hungary's political shift opened up a route for dissatisfied East Germans to enter West Germany and thus precipitated **the fall of the Berlin Wall**. As the wall was a major symbol of the **East-West political divide**, its demolition was vital in increasing the momentum for anti-communist ideals, and by July 1991 the Warsaw Pact, the communist bloc's equivalent to NATO, was dissolved and the Soviet Union was no more.

Something To Think About ...

After the Second World War Germany was divided into East and West. East Germany followed the socio-political ideologies of the communist Soviet Union, while West Germany followed the democratic principles of the West. The Berlin Wall, which divided the two countries, was a physical symbol of what Winston Churchill called the 'Iron Curtain' that separated Europe after 1945.

Former Soviet Union countries *(by population percentage)*

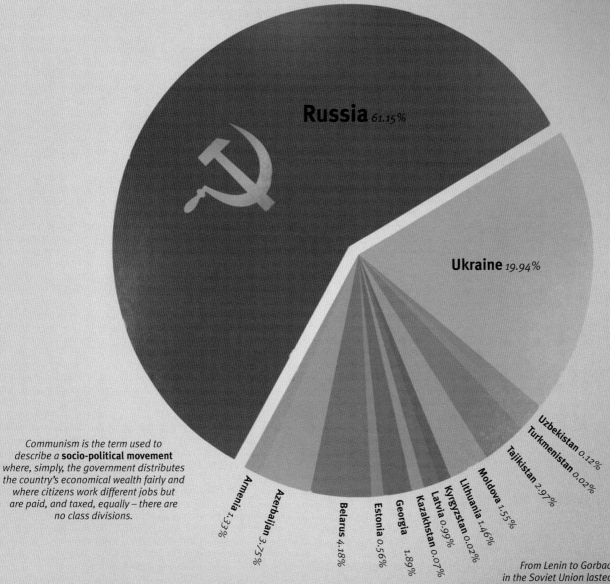

Russia *61.15%*

Ukraine *19.94%*

Uzbekistan *0.12%*

Turkmenistan *0.02%*

Tajikistan *2.97%*

Moldova *1.55%*

Lithuania *1.46%*

Kyrgyzstan *0.02%*

Latvia *0.99%*

Kazakhstan *0.07%*

Georgia *1.89%*

Estonia *0.56%*

Belarus *4.18%*

Azerbaijan *3.75%*

Armenia *1.33%*

*Communism is the term used to describe a **socio-political movement** where, simply, the government distributes the country's economical wealth fairly and where citizens work different jobs but are paid, and taxed, equally – there are no class divisions.*

*From Lenin to Gorbachev, communism in the Soviet Union lasted 74 years and played a vital role in saving the world from the Nazis, but its **political principles** were also responsible for the slaughter of up to 50 million of its own citizens, mainly while Stalin was leader (1924–53).*

The Countercultural Revolution_

The movement referred to as **'counterculture'** covers a period from the late 1950s to the early 1970s when the disaffected youth of America, Britain and other western European countries **rebelled against the establishment**. Whilst the movement didn't lead to any actual changes in government it did have long lasting effects on politics. It also led to important developments in many areas of life from art and fashion through to music and technology.

No single event led to the rise of 'counterculture', but rather a growing feeling that those in power could not be trusted, combined with a rejection of the restraints imposed as a result of post-war shortages.

In the USA, this dissatisfaction manifested itself in the form of protests supporting the **Civil Rights Movement**, opposing the Vietnam War, pushing for a growth in feminism, gay pride and appeals for free speech.

Across Europe it was students who acted as the frontline of the counterculture movement. This reached its height with the **student revolt in Paris in 1968**, the closest any of the activities came to regime change. Underlying, and possibly weakening, the legitimacy of the movement's aims, was the prevalence of drug use, mainly in the form of LSD and marijuana.

At a time when global communication was becoming more accessible and convenient the world became a melting pot for ideas so that the movement was influenced by figures that would become icons for years to come. The list is wide-ranging, and internationally eclectic, and includes Malcolm X, Martin Luther King, The Beatles, Gandhi, Che Guevara and John F. Kennedy.

Something To Think About ...

During research into analeptics – drugs that stimulate the central nervous system – LSD-25 was first synthesised in 1938 by Dr Albert Hoffman in Basel, Switzerland. Initially he discarded it as useless. It was not until five years later that he revisited it and discovered its mind-altering qualities. It then became the drug of the 1960s hippy culture.

Social Revolution
Between 1963 and 1973, the USA and UK undergoes a massive social transformation with young people rebelling against conservative social norms and questioning the authority of government. The phrase 'power to the people' becomes common and the middle of the decade sees the rise of 'hippy' culture, art-house cinema and heavy rock music, with the Woodstock Festival taking place in 1969.

Anti-War Movement
In 1969, newly elected President Richard Nixon promises to end the Vietnam War, a conflict that had divided America and had continued for many years, despite doubts over what was actually being fought for. It finally ends in 1975.

The Cold War
A state of military tension between the USA and the Soviet Union that began in the aftermath of the Second World War and is ongoing.

Nuclear Emergency
The Soviet Union has been collaborating with Cuba on building bases within arm's reach of the USA. As a result, the Cuban Missile Crisis of October 1962 is one of the main confrontations between the Soviet Union and USA during the Cold War, causing huge social distress.

Civil Rights
On 21 February 1965, African-American Muslim human rights activist Malcolm X – a spokesperson for racially equality in the USA – is assassinated before giving a speech on Afro-American unity.

Space Adventures
In 1961 President John F. Kennedy declares that by the end of the decade a manned spacecraft would land on the Moon. It does, on 20 July 1969.

Sexual Revolution
In 1960, the Food and Drug Administration in USA approves the first female birth control contraceptive pill. This aids the radicalisation of the previously taboo subject of sex in the western world, as well changing social attitudes towards a woman's role in modern society.

Women's Rights
Until the 1960s a woman's place was believed to be in the home, as wife and mother. This changes in 1963, when the Equal Pay Act in the UK breaks down the final legal barrier for a women's right to work and be paid fairly. By 1968, 'Women's Liberation' has become a household phrase, and the successful breaking down of barriers for equality in the workplace carries on into the 1990s.

Drug Culture
With the rise of youth culture and anti-authoritarian behaviour, it isn't long before drug use escalates among teenagers. With drugs like LSD and marijuana popular among the new wave of musicians and artists in the USA and UK, such as The Beatles and The Rolling Stones, drug culture expands into other areas of mainstream culture including fashion and film, with people being encouraged to 'tune in, turn on and drop out'.

The Modern Family_

Ever since *Homo sapiens* evolved, humans have lived together in **family units**. The size and function of these units has varied over the centuries but the basis has remained the same: two parents and their children. If one of the reasons why human beings simply exist at all is to **continue our species' existence** then the family unit has proved to be a very successful way of achieving this.

Before the Industrial Revolution in the 19th Century and mass transportation links, generations of families would all stay in close proximity, creating an extended family unit. As work and industry became concentrated in the **major conurbations**, people had to, or chose to, relocate to find work, and the extended family unit has given way to the simpler **nuclear family**.

When divorce and single parenthood became more common and socially acceptable in the 1960s and 1970s a new phenomenon arose. It is now common for divorced parents to take their existing family and join it with another so that there is a string of connected **nuclear units**, with siblings and half-siblings stretching across a single generation but with vastly wide age differences. The 1980s and 1990s also saw a doubling in the number of **single parent families** and a small increase in the number of married or cohabiting couples who chose not to have children. In the early 21st Century there has also been a surprising shift back to households where children remain living with their parents well into adulthood.

Something To Think About ...

In a 2002 census taken by the Census Bureau in the USA, five billion more people now inhabit the world than in 1800. In fact, in the year 2002 alone, the world gained two people per second, that's 200,000 more people per day and 6.2 million per month.

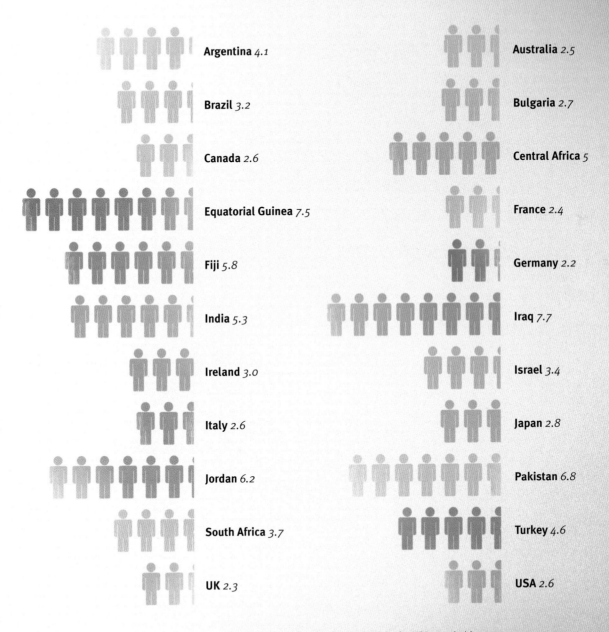

Global Average Household Size 2010 *(in persons)*

Argentina *4.1*

Brazil *3.2*

Canada *2.6*

Equatorial Guinea *7.5*

Fiji *5.8*

India *5.3*

Ireland *3.0*

Italy *2.6*

Jordan *6.2*

South Africa *3.7*

UK *2.3*

Australia *2.5*

Bulgaria *2.7*

Central Africa *5*

France *2.4*

Germany *2.2*

Iraq *7.7*

Israel *3.4*

Japan *2.8*

Pakistan *6.8*

Turkey *4.6*

USA *2.6*

*Every five minutes 67 babies are born in the USA, 274 babies
are born in China and 395 babies are born in India.*

The World Since 9/11_

The events of **September 11 2001** changed the world. When two commercial aircraft flew into, and brought down, the twin towers of The World Trade Center in New York, a dividing line was drawn in history so that we now think of the time 'Before-9/11' and 'Post-9/11' as two separate periods, almost as distinct as BC and AD. The total number of people killed on that day stands at 2,819, a tragedy on a scale a city in peacetime had never before suffered.

We live in an **economic world** and an event such as 9/11 will impact destructively upon the global stock markets. Indeed, the **Financial Times and Stock Exchange** (or FTSE) – a share index of the 100 most highly capitalised UK companies listed on the London Stock Exchange – saw an immediate dip following the terror attacks on 9/11, followed by a short spike. What this says about our world is open to debate. Did it affect us at all?

In the aftermath of 9/11, there was a US led **invasion of Iraq** where there have been over 100,000 civilian deaths. While this war continues to rage on in the region, the rest of the world continues to turn and go about its business.

This graph shows how various world events have affected the FTSE 100 share index

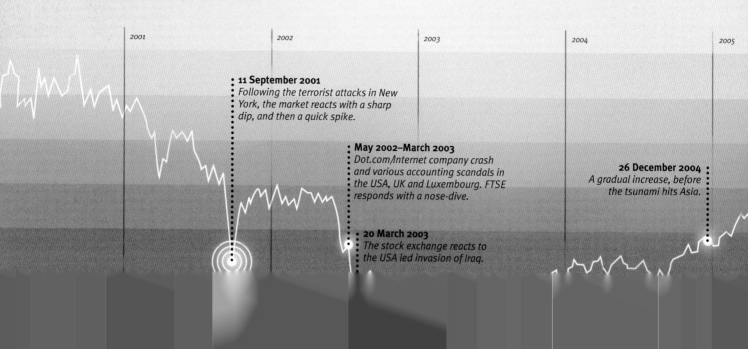

2001   2002   2003   2004   2005

11 September 2001
Following the terrorist attacks in New York, the market reacts with a sharp dip, and then a quick spike.

May 2002–March 2003
Dot.com/Internet company crash and various accounting scandals in the USA, UK and Luxembourg. FTSE responds with a nose-dive.

26 December 2004
A gradual increase, before the tsunami hits Asia.

20 March 2003
The stock exchange reacts to the USA led invasion of Iraq.

Something To Think About ...

On October 26, 2001 the then US President, George W. Bush, signed into
law the USA PATRIOT Act. As an acronym the individual letters stand for
Uniting and Strengthening America by Providing Appropriate Tools Required
to Intercept and Obstruct Terrorism. Immediately after 9/11, the people and
government of the USA were united against crimes of terrorism, but since the
act has been instigated it has come under fire for breaching the privacy and
civil liberties of many Americans as well as foreigners.

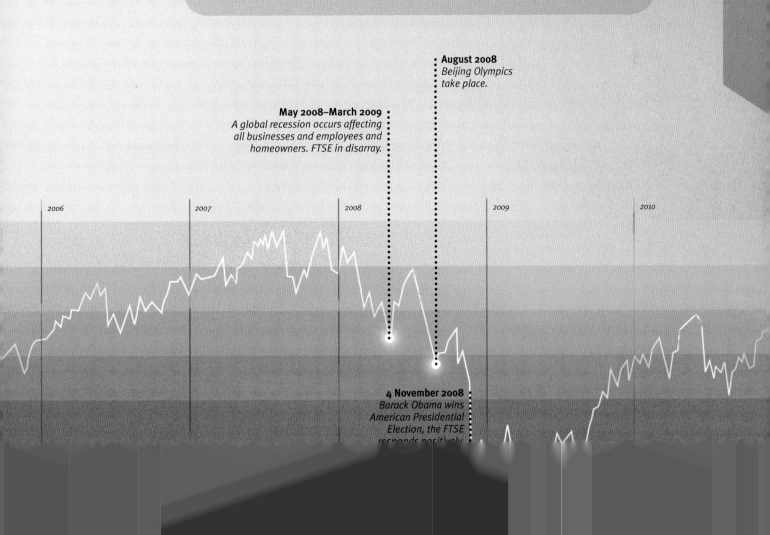

August 2008
*Beijing Olympics
take place.*

May 2008–March 2009
*A global recession occurs affecting
all businesses and employees and
homeowners. FTSE in disarray.*

2006   2007   2008   2009   2010

4 November 2008
*Barack Obama wins
American Presidential
Election, the FTSE
responds positively.*

Chapter 07.0 **Science & Medicine_**

The Size Of Atoms_

Atoms are everywhere and *everything*. You are made up of and surrounded by them. This page contains billions of them and there are trillions more of them everywhere you look. However, they are very small. So microscopic that even in the dot above this letter 'i' you could fit billions of them.

Atoms join together to form other things. One of the most well known examples of this is the combination of an **atom of oxygen** joining up with the **two atoms of hydrogen**. Together these create water – **H_2O**. When atoms combine they create **molecules**. Molecules cannot combine randomly though, because the way they bind together affects what they create, in the same way that sticking four wooden legs, a seat and a back-rest together only creates a chair if assembled correctly.

Something To Think About...

A proton's mass is the same, essentially, as that of a neutron. A proton's mass, however, is 1,840 times greater than the mass of an electron.

An atom is the basic **chemical building block** of all *matter,* everything *that we see, hear, touch and smell. Atoms* are *life.*

Atoms are made up of **protons** *(carrying positive electric charge),* **neutrons** *(no electric charge)* and **electrons** *(a negative electric charge).*

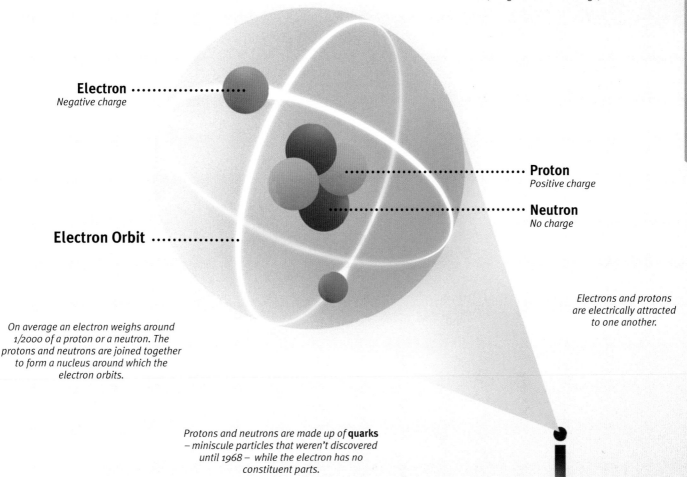

Electron
Negative charge

Proton
Positive charge

Neutron
No charge

Electron Orbit

Electrons and protons are electrically attracted to one another.

On average an electron weighs around 1/2000 of a proton or a neutron. The protons and neutrons are joined together to form a nucleus around which the electron orbits.

Protons and neutrons are made up of **quarks** *– miniscule particles that weren't discovered until 1968 – while the electron has no constituent parts.*

If a hydrogen atom were 1cm (2/5in) in diameter the electron's orbit would be 500m (1,640ft) away!

Newton's Gravity_

You can't see it, you can't touch it, but without gravity we'd all be floating around in space. The force of gravity holds us, keeps us on the surface of the Earth, and keeps the planet in a stable orbit around the Sun and generally keeps the universe in order.

Sir Isaac Newton is best known for his, probably apocryphal, observation of **an apple falling from a tree**. Seeing the fruit fall, or not, led him to come up with his *Universal Law of Gravitation*, which he explained in his *Principia* in 1687. The law states, simply, that everything attracts everything else. The strength of the force of attraction can be calculated if you know the objects' masses and the distance between them.

Newton's law remained from when the *Principia* was published until Albert Einstein came along in the early 20th Century. Published in 1915, **Einstein's Theory of General Relativity** proposed that their warping of space-time caused the apparent attraction of objects. This showed that two objects that one would expect to travel in straight lines without getting closer to one another, followed those lines but did become closer, because the straight lines became curved.

Newton's theory, and its accompanying equation, is simpler and still used today but Einstein's theory remains dominant because it explains certain anomalies not covered by Newton.

Something To Think About ...

In a vacuum, all objects are affected by gravity in the same way.
So a ping-pong ball and a cannon ball would, when thrown,
fall to the ground at the same speed.

Gravitational Constant ......

Mass of first object

Gravitational Force .....

...... Mass of second object

$$F = \frac{G m_1 m_2}{r^2}$$

Distance between the two objects

The Periodic Table Of Elements_

The chemical elements are the **building blocks** of everything we see around us. The elements themselves cannot be broken down any further and everything we know about our lives and the Universe is built from them. The atoms which form each element are attributed to an **atomic number** based on the **number of protons in the atom's nucleus.**

Russian chemist Dmitri Mendeleev is credited with creating the Periodic Table, as we now know it, in 1869. Mendeleev placed the elements in rows in order of their atomic number and started a new row when an element's properties were repeated, hence the term 'periodic'. Looking at the columns of the table enables the grouping of elements by their properties. This arrangement was his first groundbreaking discovery. His second was when he realised that the table had some gaps and that these gaps represented elements that had not yet been discovered. When he first drew up the table there were only 65 known elements. There are now 118.

In the table, as well as its atomic number, each element has a corresponding symbol (for instance **hydrogen** is 'H' and **tin** is 'Sn'), and an atomic mass. The table is used in all aspects of science and is an invaluable resource. Because elements in the same groups behave and react similarly, it allows scientists to predict the reaction even of unknown elements.

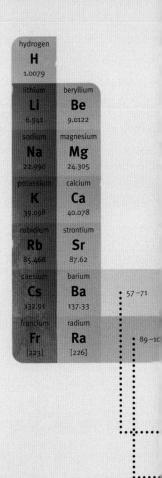

Something To Think About ...

Element 117 is currently called Ununseptium (Latin for the number 117). Its discovery has not yet been confirmed, but because there is a gap in the table, it shows there *must* be something there.

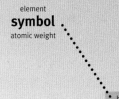

element
symbol
atomic weight

	helium
	He
	4.0026

boron	carbon	nitrogen	oxygen	flourine	neon
B	**C**	**N**	**O**	**F**	**Ne**
10.811	12.011	14.007	15.999	18.998	20.180

aluminium	silicon	phosphorus	sulphur	chlorine	argon
Al	**Si**	**P**	**S**	**Cl**	**Ar**
26.982	28.086	30.974	32.065	35.453	39.948

dium	titanium	vanadium	chromium	manganese	iron	cobalt	nickel	copper	zinc	gallium	germanium	arsenic	selenium	bromine	krypton
c	**Ti**	**V**	**Cr**	**Mn**	**Fe**	**Co**	**Ni**	**Cu**	**Zn**	**Ga**	**Ge**	**As**	**Se**	**Br**	**Kr**
956	47.867	50.942	1.996	54.938	55.845	58.933	58.693	63.546	65.39	69.723	72.61	74.922	78.96	79.904	83.80

ium	zirconium	niobium	molybdenum	technetium	ruthenium	rhodium	palladium	silver	cadmium	indium	tin	antimony	tellurium	iodine	xenon
Y	**Zr**	**Nb**	**Mo**	**Tc**	**Ru**	**Rh**	**Pd**	**Ag**	**Cd**	**In**	**Sn**	**Sb**	**Te**	**I**	**Xe**
906	91.224	92.906	95.94	[98]	101.07	102.91	106.42	107.87	112.41	114.82	118.71	121.76	127.60	126.90	131.29

tium	hafnium	tantalum	tungsten	rhenium	osmium	iridium	platinum	gold	mercury	thallium	lead	bismuth	polonium	astatine	radon
u	**Hf**	**Ta**	**W**	**Re**	**Os**	**Ir**	**Pt**	**Au**	**Hg**	**Tl**	**Pb**	**Bi**	**Po**	**At**	**Rn**
.97	178.49	180.95	183.94	186.21	190.23	192.22	195.08	196.97	200.59	204.38	207.2	208.98	[209]	[210]	[222]

ncium	rutherfordium	dubnium	seaborgium	bohrium	hassium	meitnerium	ununnillum	unununium	ununbium	ununtrium	ununquadium	ununpentium	ununhexium	ununseptium	ununoctium
r	**Rf**	**Db**	**Sg**	**Bh**	**Hs**	**Mt**	**Uun**	**Uuu**	**Uub**	**Uut**	**Uuq**	**Uup**	**Uuh**	**Uus**	**Uuo**
52]	[261]	[262]	[266]	[264]	[269]	[268]	[271]	[272]	[277]	[286]	[289]	[289]	[293]	[294]	[294]

lanthanum	cerium	prasedymium	neodymium	promethium	samarium	europium	gadolinium	terbium	dysprosium	holmium	erbium	thulium	ytterbium
La	**Ce**	**Pr**	**Nd**	**Pm**	**Sm**	**Eu**	**Gd**	**Tb**	**Dy**	**Ho**	**Er**	**Tm**	**Yb**
138.91	140.12	140.91	144.24	[145]	150.36	151.96	157.25	158.93	162.50	164.93	167.26	168.93	173.04

actinium	thorium	protactinium	uranium	neptunium	plutonium	americium	curium	berkelium	californium	einsteinium	fermium	mendelevium	nobelium
Ac	**Th**	**Pa**	**U**	**Np**	**Pu**	**Am**	**Cm**	**Bk**	**Cf**	**Es**	**Fm**	**Md**	**No**
[227]	232.04	231.04	238.03	[237]	[244]	[243]	[247]	[247]	888	[252]	[257]	[258]	[259]

- Alkali metals
- Alkaline earth metals
- Lanthanides
- Actinides
- Transition elements
- Poor metals
- Metalloids
- Other non-metals
- Halogens
- Noble gases
- Unknown chemical properties

07.4 Equations You Need To Know_

All the sciences rely on mathematics to help them make sense of the world and everything we do can be illustrated or explained using mathematics. Whether it is working out how long we will have to wait for the next bus or predicting when an asteroid may hit Earth, **mathematics is vital**.

Early mathematics was purely to do with the everyday elements of life such as commerce and farming but once it was realised that mathematics could be used to describe the world we live in, and even predict outcomes, its **possibilities became infinite**. There is a beauty and simplicity to mathematics which does not exist in the other sciences. The **Golden Ratio** is an example of mathematics crossing over into another discipline and setting a standard for it.

The Golden Ratio applies in art all the time: it states that a line with a total length $a + b$ is to the length of the longer segment a as the length of a is to the length of the shorter segment b. This ratio is seen in many classic works of art for instance the 'Mona Lisa'. The ratio of the height of her face to the width is the Golden Ratio, as is her forehead's width and height, as displayed in the ratio below:

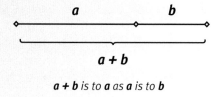

a + b is to *a* as *a* is to *b*

Something To Think About ...

Zero (0) was invented as early as the 5th century by mathematicians in India. Zero was used repeatedly when looking at stars and gauging distances. In Europe, before 0 had travelled the world, all Europeans used Roman numerals to do calculations, although this made it difficult as Roman numerals use symbols, and have obvious limitations when dealing with lots of numbers.

Equation 1
Pi

$$\pi = \frac{C}{d}$$

C: circumference of a circle

d: diameter of a circle

π: Pi

Equation 2
Albert Einstein's Theory of General Relativity

$$E = mc^2$$

E: energy

m: mass

c: the speed of light

Equation 3
Sir Isaac Newton's Second Law of Mechanics

$$F = ma$$

F: force

m: mass

a: acceleration

Equation 4
Pythagoras' Theorem

$$a^2 + b^2 = c^2$$

a and b: the two shortest sides of a right angled triangle

c: the long side

Equation 5
Repaying your mortgage

C: loan amount

N: number of months

$$P = \frac{Cr(1+r)^N}{(1+r)^N - 1}$$

P: monthly payment

r: monthly interest (1/12 of annual rate)

Equation 6
Area of a circle

$$A = \pi r^2$$

A: area

π: Pi

r: radius

177

How Electricity Works_

Around the **nucleus** of every atom there are **electrons** that move around the nucleus. When the electrons are given 'energy' by a power source, they jump from one atom to the next. This movement is an **electric current**. It is this current, or **movement of electrons**, that makes electrical objects work. The vital element that electricity needs is a completed circuit. When we flick a light switch, we are completing a circuit that allows the electrons to move and this is what makes the bulb light up.

In the wire that makes up most of the circuit the electrons can move freely, without much resistance, like water through a wide pipe, but when they reach the light bulb and its filament – the part that lights up – the **resistance is high**, as though the pipe is too narrow. It is this resistance, and the strain it puts on the movement of the electrons, which **heats up the filament** and makes the bulb glow.

Something To Think About ...

Italian physicist Alessandro Volta is credited with inventing the first electric battery, but this discovery only came about thanks indirectly to experiments carried out on frogs' legs by contemporary Luigi Galvani, and the realisation that their muscles twitched when an electric charge was introduced.

An electric current always finds the easiest path to the ground.

Electricity is created when electrons move from atom to atom.

Electricity travels at 300,000 kilometres per second. If a human being could travel that fast it could travel around the world eight times in the time it takes to switch on a light bulb.

Your brain generates between 10 and 25 watts of power – just enough to power a light bulb.

Current flow

Electron flow

Switch
Off/On

**Battery/
Source**

*A power source can be either direct current or alternating current.
A battery is an example of the former and the charge is caused by a chemical reaction.
A power station creates alternating current due to the movement
of a magnet within a copper coil.*

179

The Inside Life Of Bacteria_

The bacteria that exist on and around us today began their evolution when the Earth first began. Bacteria are **single-celled organisms** and have the basic structure that would have been found in the very first organisms from which everything eventually evolved. In essence, they were the **very first life forms** to develop on Earth.

Bacteria have a reputation for being harmful. In fact there are more **helpful bacteria** types, than harmful. For instance, the bacteria located in the human gut are vital in digestion, producing vitamins and stimulating our immune system.

Bacterial infection develops when the bacteria gain access to the body's tissue. The site of access is generally through the mouth, nose and eyes but can also be via wounds. These infections can, if left to run their course, cause plagues and **death on a large scale** (such as the Black Death which killed up to 77 million people between 1348 and 1350 in Europe) but the development of anti-bacterial drugs – **antibiotics** – has helped us to reduce these epidemic incidents. Before antibiotics became readily available, chemist Louis Pasteur discovered in 1864 that the process of boiling kills all known bacteria, hence the term **Pasteurisation**.

Something To Think About ...

Dutchman, and the first microbiologist, Antony van Leeuwenhoek, was the first person to 'see' bacteria. He pioneered high-powered microscopes to look at, among many other things, pond water, where he first saw bacteria.

The structure of a bacterial cell

Bacteria are split into two groups; **bacteria** *and* **cyanobacteria**. *Cyanobacteria are responsible for the creation of our oxygen-rich atmosphere.*

Bacteria come in three shapes: **sphere** *(coccus),* **rod** *(bacillus) or* **spiral** *(spirillum).*

Capsule

Cell wall

Plasma membrane

Bacteria can survive and thrive at a massive range of temperatures.

Ribosomes

Cytoplasm

Nucleoid

Pili

Bacterial Flagellum

Antibiotics, such as the most common, Penicillin, interfere with the insides of a bacterial cell and stop it from multiplying.

Bacteria are small, **very** *small. They are roughly 1,000 nanometres in size. A nanometre is one millionth of a millimeter.*

There are more bacterial cells in our bodies than human cells. There are even more bacterial cells in our body than there are people on the planet!

07.7 The Rules Of Magnetic Attraction_

A magnet is an object or material that produces a **magnetic field**. Our planet, Earth, is a magnet. All magnets have a north pole and a south pole. The rule of magnetism is: u*nlike poles* **attract**, *like poles* **repel**.

The magnetic field is created by the **movement of electrons** within the magnet. The fact that the magnetism comes from this action also links magnets to electricity, in what we call **electromagnetism**. They are two sides of the same coin.

There are two types of magnet, **permanent** and **electro**. In the former, the magnetic field is fixed and will always be in operation. In the electromagnet, the magnetic field is only operational when the current is flowing. These different properties mean that different jobs are best performed by one type or the other. The magnet that holds notes on to your fridge is an example of a permanent magnet. Electromagnets are found in most machines that we use regularly, for example, cars, stereos, televisions and computers.

When an **electric current** flows along a wire a magnetic field is created and when you spin a magnet within a wire coil you get an electric current. Knowing this, and a little about electrons (which orbit around the nucleus of an atom), explains how a magnetic field can be created without an apparent electric current.

Something To Think About ...

In Shanghai, China, a train called a Maglev uses magnetic levitation – the process by which magnets are used to make objects float – to transport people around. The train can travel, on average, around 250km/h (160mph) – much faster than conventional track-dependent trains.

Earth's magnetic power comes from its liquid centre causing it to be a massive electromagnet.

The magnetic pull is always strongest at the poles.

Magnetic attraction works at great distances, and even in a vacuum such as Space.

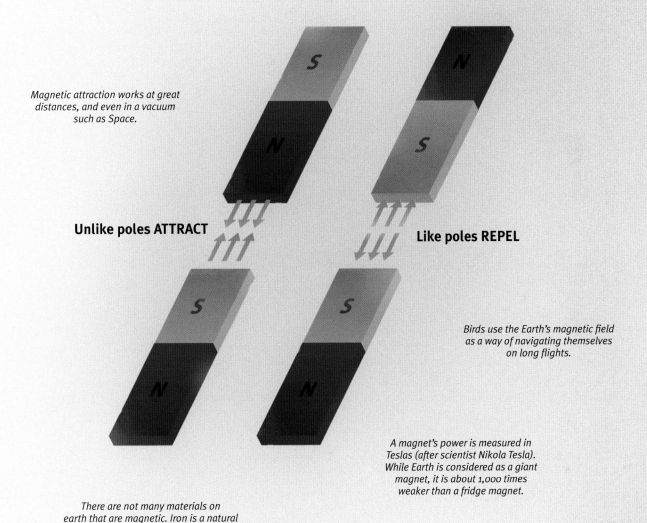

Unlike poles ATTRACT

Like poles REPEL

Birds use the Earth's magnetic field as a way of navigating themselves on long flights.

A magnet's power is measured in Teslas (after scientist Nikola Tesla). While Earth is considered as a giant magnet, it is about 1,000 times weaker than a fridge magnet.

There are not many materials on earth that are magnetic. Iron is a natural magnetic metal but other, principal, metals are nickel, cobalt and steel.

The Unique History Of Measurement_

Three of the main dimensions that we measure are **distance, weight,** and **time**. They are all made up of finite units and these units have become standardised around the world. One **second** in Boston, England is the same length of time as one second in Boston, Massachusetts, USA. One **kilogramme** in Madrid is the same as one kilogramme in Manchester, and one **metre** is the same on Long Island as it is in Littlehampton. This is vital so that around the globe when you order 4kg of flour to be delivered in three days the people you are ordering from know what you mean.

Today's **Metric System** owes much to the French Revolution of 1789–99 and Louis XVI. The French monarch ordered that a **new system of measurement** be developed to provide something more **universally applicable** than what had previously been used.

Something To Think About ...

Every 30 million years even the world's most accurate clocks, such as NIST-F1 at the American National Institute of Standards and Technology, Maryland, will gain or lose one second in time.

**Comparing the origin of measurements
to how they are calculated now**

Historic   New

This was based on the apparent movement
of the Sun around the Earth. A solar day was
divided by 24 (into hours), these were divided
by 60 (into minutes) and each minute further
divided by 60 to give the length of a second.

A second

Since 1967, a second has been defined as
the duration of 9,192,631,770 periods of
the radiation corresponding to the transition
between the two hyperfine levels of the ground
state of the caesium 133 atom.

A metre was originally defined as
1/10,000,000 of the distance from the
North Pole to the Equator.

A metre

A metre is the length of the path travelled
by light in a vacuum during a time interval
of 1/299,792,458 of a second. The word
'metre' was introduced into the English
Language in 1797.

Three barleycorns
After 1606, barleycorns were
used as they are uniform
in length –8mm.

An inch

2.54cm

The mass of a litre of
water at 0°C.

A kilogramme

Equal to the mass of the international prototype
of the kilogramme, which is a cylinder made of an
alloy for which the mass fraction of platinum is
90% and the mass fraction of iridium is 10%.

7,200 wheat grains

A pound

0.45359237kg

The Medical Trade_

When we are ill and want to get better we take medicine. The word medicine covers a multitude of treatments but they all fall into three different areas in terms of how they work.

- **Replacing a deficiency** – *Supplement*
- **Killing an intruder** – *Assassin*
- **Changing the behaviour of the cells** – *Modifier*

Supplement

Rickets, a softening of the bones that can lead to fractures and deformity, is an example of a deficiency disease and can be treated with a combination of Vitamin D, Calcium and sunlight.

Assassin

Bacterial infections are a major cause of illness and Penicillin is probably the most well-known and commonly used treatment. Penicillin was discovered by accident in 1928 by Alexander Fleming. At its most basic level penicillin works by breaking down the cell walls of bacteria.

Modifier

Ibuprofen, like most modifiers, does not actually cure you of the illness, but it will dampen down the symptoms, often completely. By inhibiting cyclooxygenase, an enzyme responsible for producing pain signals, Ibuprofen effectively tricks the body into thinking it is not in pain.

As well as the three methods of operation it is important to consider the delivery method, Drugs are carried around the body by the blood and thus the speed of absorption into the blood will affect a treatment's efficacy.

- **Intravenous** – *introduced directly into the blood*
- **Intramuscular** – *introduced directly into a muscle*
- **Subcutaneous** – *introduced just under the skin*
- **Rectal** – *introduced through the bowel*
- **Oral** – *taken by swallowing*

The choice depends on the type of medicine, the illness involved and the speed and period of delivery required. It might seem that you would always want delivery to be as quick as possible but some treatments need a slow long release, such as insulin for diabetes.

Something To Think About ...

Non-prescription drugs such as alcohol, caffeine and nicotine are still the most abused drugs in the world. Over 450,000,000 cups of coffee are drunk in the USA every day (that's 1 and a half cups for every man, woman and child) and a 10g dose of caffeine is considered lethal.

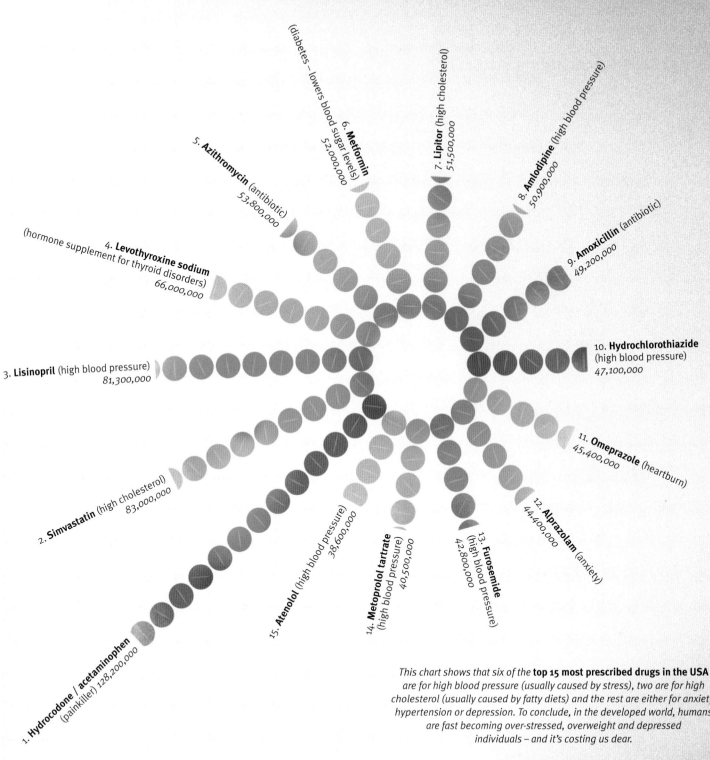

5. **Azithromycin** (antibiotic)
53,800,000

(diabetes – lowers blood sugar levels)
6. **Metformin**
52,000,000

7. **Lipitor** (high cholesterol)
54,500,000

8. **Amlodipine** (high blood pressure)
50,900,000

4. **Levothyroxine sodium**
(hormone supplement for thyroid disorders)
66,000,000

9. **Amoxicillin** (antibiotic)
49,200,000

3. **Lisinopril** (high blood pressure)
81,300,000

10. **Hydrochlorothiazide**
(high blood pressure)
47,100,000

11. **Omeprazole** (heartburn)
45,400,000

2. **Simvastatin** (high cholesterol)
83,000,000

12. **Alprazolam** (anxiety)
44,400,000

13. **Furosemide**
(high blood pressure)
42,800,000

15. **Atenolol** (high blood pressure)
38,600,000

14. **Metoprolol tartrate**
(high blood pressure)
40,500,000

1. **Hydrocodone / acetaminophen**
(painkiller) 128,200,000

This chart shows that six of the **top 15 most prescribed drugs in the USA**
are for high blood pressure (usually caused by stress), two are for high
cholesterol (usually caused by fatty diets) and the rest are either for anxiety,
hypertension or depression. To conclude, in the developed world, humans
are fast becoming over-stressed, overweight and depressed
individuals – and it's costing us dear.

What's Killing Us?

There are many ways for human beings to die and as we have evolved we have learned ways to avoid it for longer. It is true to say that because of the way we live now, the things that kill us, or at least make us ill, have changed as well. It is even possible to prove that we are now being brought down by diseases that previously would not have affected us, simply because we are living longer and giving the diseases more opportunity to attack us.

The World Health Organisation, when looking at the causes of death, has three main categories: a) **non-communicable conditions**, b) **communicable diseases**, maternal and perinatal conditions and nutritional deficiencies and c) **injuries**. In their latest figures these account for a) 58.65%, b) 32.31% and c) 9.04%.

The single biggest killer, globally, is **cardiovascular disease**, which accounts for nearly 30% of deaths annually. Cancer in all its various forms takes 12.46% and HIV/AIDS is responsible for just over 5%. Amazingly, road traffic accidents kill over 2% but war is only responsible for 0.3%, whilst intentional self-inflicted injuries cause 1.53% of deaths.

The major difference in the developed world between now and the 19th Century, was the **discovery of antibiotics**, especially Penicillin. During the 19th Century bacterial disease was rife. The top killers in those days were pneumonia, tuberculosis, diphtheria, and typhoid.

Something To Think About ...

Even if disease doesn't kill us, humans will still age and die. This ageing is due to the deterioration of a protective cap on our chromosomes. In 2010 researchers at Harvard University in the USA reversed the signs of ageing in mice by manipulating this cap. Tests are about to start on humans ...

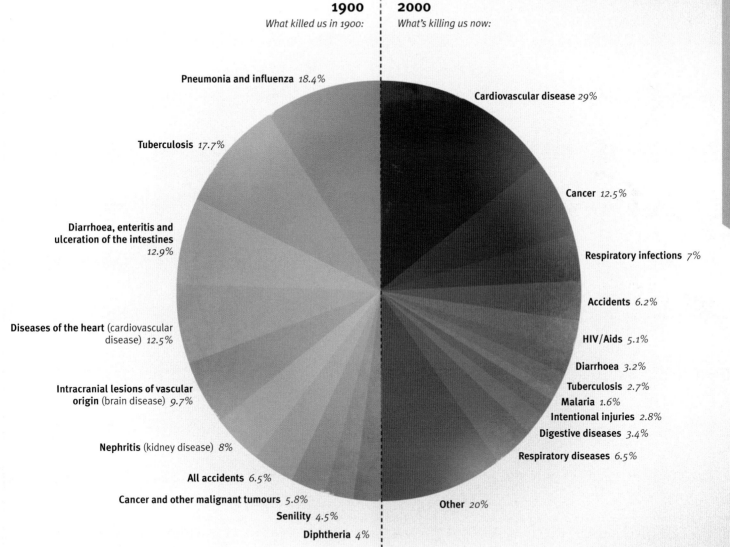

1900
What killed us in 1900:

2000
What's killing us now:

Pneumonia and influenza *18.4%*

Tuberculosis *17.7%*

Diarrhoea, enteritis and
ulceration of the intestines
12.9%

Diseases of the heart (cardiovascular
disease) *12.5%*

Intracranial lesions of vascular
origin (brain disease) *9.7%*

Nephritis (kidney disease) *8%*

All accidents *6.5%*

Cancer and other malignant tumours *5.8%*

Senility *4.5%*

Diphtheria *4%*

Cardiovascular disease *29%*

Cancer *12.5%*

Respiratory infections *7%*

Accidents *6.2%*

HIV/Aids *5.1%*

Diarrhoea *3.2%*

Tuberculosis *2.7%*

Malaria *1.6%*

Intentional injuries *2.8%*

Digestive diseases *3.4%*

Respiratory diseases *6.5%*

Other *20%*

[Figures shown are for USA, 1900 and 2000.]

189

The Speed Of Speed_

It is universally known that the fictional super-hero Superman can travel faster than a speeding bullet. That is indeed exceptionally quick. But **nothing is faster than the speed of light**. For a long time, until the mid-17th Century, most people thought that light travelled instantaneously.

It was a Danish astronomer, Ole Romer, who in 1676 first noticed that light travelled at a **finite speed**. In observing the lunar eclipses of Jupiter he realised that they happened earlier than expected when Earth was closer to Jupiter. The only explanation for this was that the light took less time to reach us and therefore could not be instantaneous.

One of the important things to note about the speed of light is that its **speed is constant**. It does not vary regardless of the source, be it the light in your fridge or the most expensive military laser. The constancy and rapidity of light speed is useful for measuring objects that are great distances away from Earth. It is common scientific practice to refer to distances in space, not by the distance in kilometres, but by the number of years it takes light to reach the object you are measuring, or a **light year**.

The speed of light is denoted as c and is a vital component in the formulation of **Einstein's theory of special relativity**.

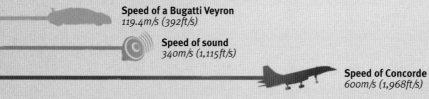

Speed of a Bugatti Veyron
119.4m/s (392ft/s)

Speed of sound
340m/s (1,115ft/s)

Speed of Concorde
600m/s (1,968ft/s)

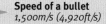

Speed of a bullet
1,500m/s (4,920ft/s)

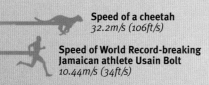

Speed of a cheetah
32.2m/s (106ft/s)

Speed of World Record-breaking Jamaican athlete Usain Bolt
10.44m/s (34ft/s)

0

Something To Think About...

Light travels at 1,080km/h (671,000,000 miles) per hour. To us that feels instantaneous. In the context of space, it's rather slow. If you were to have a conversation with an astronaut on Mars it would take the radio signals – travelling at the speed of light – 42 minutes to arrive on Earth.

Speed of light
299,792,458m/s (983,319,262ft/s)

Speed of the Space Shuttle Endeavour
8,000m/s (26,240ft/s)

1 second

Science And Medicine's Finest Hours_

It is obvious, from the world we see around us everyday, that there have been many **amazing advances** in the worlds of science and medicine since human beings have been able to think independently. It is often the case, however, that the scientists, mathematicians and doctors we associate with a particular development in these fields were not necessarily the first to make that discovery. They were just the best at communicating their find.

What is not in doubt is that any new discovery in a field makes development that much easier. It is this development that explains the exponential growth in **the speed of human advancement and achievement**. This growth can be described using the **Fibonacci sequence**, explained in 1202 by Leonardo of Pisa.

580 BC
Pythagoras born in Samos, Greece.

460 BC
Hippocrates, the father of medicine is born in Kos, Greece.

1202
Leonardo of Pisa posits the Fibonacci sequence.

1543
Polish astronomer Nicolaus Copernicus proposes a heliocentric view of the Solar System.

1687
Isaac Newton publishes Philosophiae Naturalis Principia Mathematica.

1749
The father of immunology, Edward Jenner, born in Berkeley, Gloucestershire.

1802
British scientist John Dalton discovers the atom.

1804
First surgery under anaesthetic performed by Japanese surgeon

Something To Think About…

The Fibonacci sequence, whilst a mathematical construct, is often found in nature. 1, 1, 2, 3, 5, 8, 13, 21, 34, 55, 89, and so on. One example is the spiral on a snail's shell.

1818
Dr James Blundell performs the first successful blood transfusion in London.

1842
American physician Crawford Long uses ether as a general anaesthetic.

1850s–60s
Louis Pasteur (France) and Robert Koch (Prussia) establish the germ theory of disease.

1860
Florence Nightingale establishes a training school for nurses.

1897
Aspirin, the wonder drug, developed in Germany by chemist Felix Hoffmann.

1928
Penicillin discovered by Scottish biologist Alexander Fleming.

1967
First heart transplant performed by South African heart surgeon Christiaan Barnard.

1983
HIV (the AIDS virus) is identified.

2010
First full face transplant takes place in Spain.

1821
British mathematician and inventor Charles Babbage designs the first computer – Difference Engine 1.

1859
Charles Darwin publishes The Origin of Species.

1895
Marconi sends a radio signal over 1.6km (1 mile).

1945
First Atomic explosion takes place in New Mexico.

1953
DNA Modelled by Crick and Watson.

1961
Russian cosmonaut Yuri Gagarin becomes the first man in space.

1990
Hubble Space Telescope is launched.

Chapter 08.0 **Technology & Communications_**

The Science Of Progress_

One of the things that distinguishes Man from all other animals on the planet is our ability to invent things. This is a by-product of the **development and evolution** of our brains over time, but also a result of the fact that we are never really satisfied with what we've got.

People often say that **modern-day innovations** and appliances are the 'greatest invention since sliced bread'. Well, sliced bread, or rather a machine to slice loaves and wrap them in wax paper, was invented in 1928. When it arrived it led to a massive increase in the consumption of bread, mainly because it was so easy to have just 'one more slice'. This had not been the motivation for the invention originally and is certainly not the only unexpected consequence of a new discovery or creation. Humankind's **first great discovery**, fire, was initially used merely for warmth, but when it began to be used to cook the meat of dead animals it had the unforeseen knock-on effect of speeding up Man's evolution.

Fire
7000 BC (estimated)

Alphabet
2700 BC

Toilet paper
14th Century China

Steam engine
*1769 – James Watt
Scotland*

Telephone
*1876 – Alexander Graham B
Canada*

Wheel
3200 BC

Clock
*1090 – Su Song
China*

Printing press
*1440 – Johannes Gutenberg
Germany*

Electricity
*1831 – Michael Faraday
England*

Something To Think About…

The Timeline, the idea of displaying simple chronological events graphically, was invented by a Swiss mathematician named Leonhard Euler (1707–83).

Television
1925 – John Logie Baird
Scotland

World Wide Web (Internet)
1989 – Tim Berners-Lee
England

Powered flight
1903 – The Wright Brothers
USA

Computer
1936 – Alan Turing
England

Automobile
1889 – Gottlieb Daimler
Germany

Sliced bread
1928 – Otto Frederick Rohwedder
USA

Electric washing machine
1906-ish (disputed)

Mobile phone
1973 – Martin Cooper (Motorola)
USA

The Evolution Of Transport_

The most important invention, or discovery, since the wheel is a coveted title.
Since evolving into *Homo sapiens*, and having the ability to create, it is also
no secret that the invention of the wheel changed life as we knew it forever.
On an average day in the 21st Century our **reliance on the wheel** is
almost absolute.

The wheel, as a circle and thus a **symbol of renewal and rebirth**, is in itself a
powerful metaphor for how this device has helped us survive and flourish.
The utilisation of this shape as a means of transporting materials,
possessions and ourselves has allowed us to conquer the Earth.

The first wheel was really not a wheel at all but hundreds of wheels all stuck
together – more commonly known as a log or tree trunk. By placing a series of trunks
under a heavy object, it was possible to move it much more easily than by merely
pushing it along the ground. The jump from this to using a slice, or thin cross-section,
of a tree was the moment when the first wheel came into existence. The addition
of a central axle around which the wheel could move came next. This step,
probably around 3,000 years ago, was in effect the last development
of the wheel.

c.4000 BC
A series of logs are rolled together; this is how
the Egyptians transported the stone that built
the Great Pyramids.

c.3807 BC
Europe's first wooden footpath,
The Sweet Track, is built near Glastonbury,
England.

c.3500 BC
Wooden log rafts with oars –
or river boats – are first used.

c.3200 BC
Wheels with axles are first produced.

c.3000 BC
Mesopotamian war chariot appears.

c.2000 BC
Horses are trained to pull carts.

312 BC
Romans lay down the first paved road
and call it The Appian Way.

234–181 BC
The wheelbarrow is invented.

700 AD
Triangular, or lateen, sails
are invented, possibly in Egypt.

770
Horseshoes are fitted to improve
transportation by horses.

852
The earliest form of parachute is invented.

1266
Compasses first appear, China.

1662
Frenchman Blaise Pascal invents
the horse-drawn coach.

1801
Richard Trevithick demonstrates
his steam train.

Something To Think About...

The Aerostat Reveillon, the first ever hot-air balloon, was launched on the 19 September 1783 by a scientist called Jean Francois Pilatre de Rozier. Onboard passengers were a cockerel, a duck and a sheep. The first manned hot-air balloon ride took place on 21 November 1783 when Joseph and Etienne Montgolfier took off from the centre of Paris. They were in the air for 20 minutes – five minutes longer than their animal counterparts.

1817
German Baron Karl von Drais invents a running bike called the Draisine.

1825
The first public passenger railway opens, the Stockton and Darlington, north-east England.

1867
The motorcycle is invented.

1870s
James Starley's Penny Farthing is invented.

1885
John Kemp Starley invents the safety bicycle – with chain.

1885
Karl Benz builds a practical automobile – the world's first.

1888
John Boyd Dunlop builds the first pneumatic tyre.

1903
Orville and Wilbur Wright pilot the first powered flight.

1919
The first daily passenger flight from London to Paris.

1947
USA's Chuck Yeagar makes his famous first supersonic jet flight.

1964
The Japanese invent the super-fast bullet train.

1969
First manned spacecraft lands on the Moon.

1970
First jumbo jet takes to the skies.

1981
NASA launches its first Space Shuttle.

2001
The personal, two-wheeled electric Segway is introduced.

The History Of The Printed Word_

The earliest method of printing was produced by carving into wood and then transferring the image on to paper by inking the wood. This was very time-consuming and complicated as whatever was being printed had to be carved in reverse.

The major leap forward came with the production of individual blocks for each letter of the alphabet and construction of a frame into which these could be placed – this was called the **printing press**. Whilst there have been improvements since Johannes Gutenberg invented his printing press in the mid-15th Century, the processes now are essentially the same except everything is done by computer.

Advances in printing technology were vital in the **dissemination of information and ideas**. In dictatorial regimes where ideas printed in books go against the ideology of the current rulers (and where they do not encourage free speech), freedom of expression via the printed word can be a dangerous weapon. If it is true that the pen is mightier than the sword, it cannot be denied that **the printing press is mightier than the pen**.

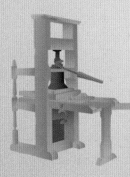

Printing Press

1041
First printing, using carved **wooden blocks** *covered in ink, transferred text and image onto paper, Bi Sheng, China.*

1241
Koreans use **metal moveable type** *to print books.*

1309
Paper first made by Europeans.

1338
In France, the first paper-mill opens.

1430
Intaglio printing *first used.*

1476
In England, **William Caxton** *uses a Gutenberg printing press.*

1501
Italic type *is first used.*

Printed Word

868 AD
Diamond Sutra *– The world's first printed book or the earliest dated printed book found so far.*

1543
Copernicus publishes his **Heavenly Spheres.**

1570
Beware the Cat *by William Baldwin – the first novel in English.*

1605
Relation *– the first weekly newspaper printed in Strasbourg by Johan Carolus.*

1611
King James **Bible** *published.*

Something To Think About ...

Louise Braille's six-dot writing system evolved from the tactile *Ecriture Nocturne* (night writing) code invented by Charles Barbier de la Serre. This code was used to send military messages that could be read on the battlefield at night without light.

1623
William Shakespeare's First Folio – *a collected edition of all his plays. Without this, there would be no Shakespeare today.*

1755
Samuel Johnson publishes the first dictionary.

1785
The Times (*as the Daily Universal Register*) *first printed. Oldest national paper in the world.*

1796
Lithography – *a type of printing using a stone or metal plate – invented by Alois Senefelder.*

1824
French teenager Louise Braille, aged 15, invents the six-dot system that now bears his name.

1903
American Ira Washington Rubel accidentally invents **offset printing,** *when he forgets to put the paper into the press and the ink goes on to the rubber cylinder. When he then inserts the paper the resulting image on the paper is clearer.*

1920 (US), **1921** (UK)
The Mysterious Affair at Styles – *Agatha Christie's first book published.*

1925
Mein Kampf – *Adolf Hitler's autobiography.*

1927
The International Federation of Library Associations and Institutions is founded – they oversee the cataloguing of all published books.

1932
Albatross Books in Germany are credited with creating **the first mass-market paperback books.**

1960
To Kill a Mockingbird *by Harper Lee – regarded as one of the best novels of all time.*

1988
Professor Stephen Hawking publishes **A Brief History of Time** – *a vital, and popular, book on the history of the Universe.*

1995
Website Amazon begins selling books.

1997
Harry Potter and the Philosopher's Stone *by J.K. Rowling (only 500 printed in first print run).*

1998
Softbook release the first type of e-book reader.

2005
The Girl with the Dragon Tattoo *by Stieg Larsson – the must-read book of the decade.*

2007
Amazon release its first generation **digital e-book reader,** *the Kindle.*

2011
Where next for the book?

The History Of Communication_

The ancient history of communication is difficult to document because we are limited to what has survived through the ages. Whilst we can make solid assumptions based on **cave drawings**, for instance, we can only guess at how verbal communication developed. Regarding other forms of communication, some researchers believe that information may have been passed on using something as simple as a piece of string with knots in, however it is impossible to know for sure as there are no surviving examples to study.

Communication, and its evolution, can be split into two areas: **oral and visual**. The former developed from basic animal noises, used as warnings or soothing sounds. As we started to walk on two feet, and our vocal chords changed shape, we were able to go beyond primitive guttural utterances.

Whilst **visual communication** may be seen as separate from oral, it is likely that it developed originally because of the limitations in our speaking. Before words had been created it is thought that drawings were used to explain things or record events. Ironically, once language had been created, much of the visual communication then became symbolic of the thing it described, rather than a true rendition of it.

It is estimated that a week's worth of news in an average newspaper contains more information than anyone in the 18th century would have learnt in their entire lifetime.

Something To Think About ...

Whilst suffering from Locked-in Syndrome, a condition in which a patient is aware and awake but cannot move or communicate verbally due to complete paralysis of nearly all voluntary muscles in the body, Jean-Dominique Bauby managed to write his autobiography, *The Diving Bell and the Butterfly*, by blinking his left eye.

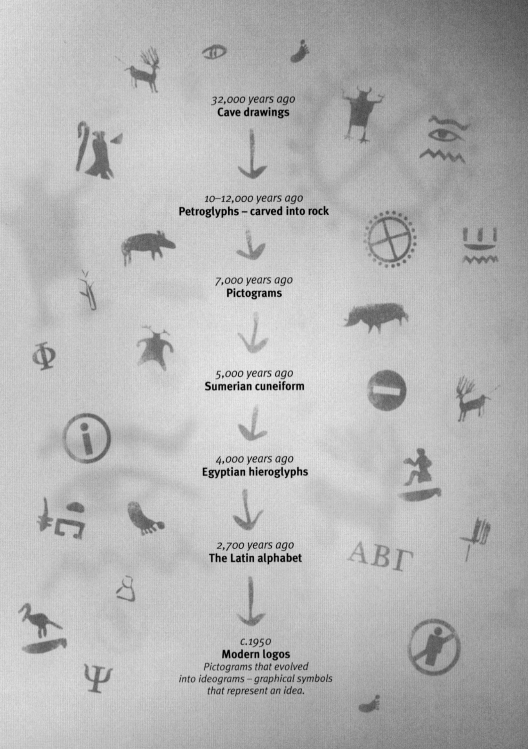

32,000 years ago
Cave drawings

10–12,000 years ago
Petroglyphs – carved into rock

7,000 years ago
Pictograms

5,000 years ago
Sumerian cuneiform

4,000 years ago
Egyptian hieroglyphs

2,700 years ago
The Latin alphabet

c.1950
Modern logos
*Pictograms that evolved
into ideograms – graphical symbols
that represent an idea.*

How A Telephone Works_

Although phones – and mobile phones – have changed quite dramatically from an aesthetic point over the past 60 years, the technology of *how they work* has essentially remained the same.

A telephone works by converting *sound waves* into an **electric current**, sending that current down a wire, and then converting it back into **sound waves**. In essence it is no different from two cans and a piece of string, but it is more efficient and can work over much longer, almost infinite, distances.

With the cans method, the vibrations in the air created by your voice make the end of the can vibrate. This minute vibration is carried by the string to the can at the other end, causing it to vibrate in the same way, thus creating the same sound waves you created by speaking. The tighter the piece of string is held the better the transmission will be.

A telephone replicates this idea. The end of the can is replaced by a **membrane** and **carbon granules**. When you speak, the **sound waves move the membrane**, which is attached to an electric circuit. The movement of the membrane changes the current in this circuit and it is this 'electrical message' that is sent down the phone wire.

When you dial a number and someone answers, in effect they are **completing an electric circuit**. This allows your 'electrical message' to travel along the wire connecting you and act on the membrane in the ear piece, reversing the process from your mouthpiece and turning the electric signal back into sound waves.

Although technology has come a long way, and we no longer have a physical wire that connects the people on either end, the principle is still exactly the same: sound waves are turned into radio signals, these are then sent to the receiver, which converts them back again.

Something To Think About...

With phone handsets halving in size every 18 months on average, scientists predict that by the year 2017 mobile phone designs will have reached the physical limits of technology.

While the look and feel of most modern mobile and smartphones may appear different to the original rotary dial telephones, much of the technology that enables a conversation to take place is almost exactly the same.

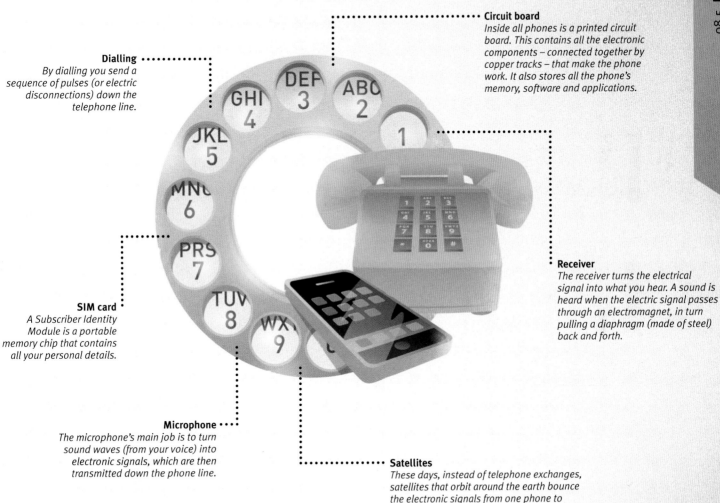

Circuit board
Inside all phones is a printed circuit board. This contains all the electronic components – connected together by copper tracks – that make the phone work. It also stores all the phone's memory, software and applications.

Dialling
By dialling you send a sequence of pulses (or electric disconnections) down the telephone line.

SIM card
A Subscriber Identity Module is a portable memory chip that contains all your personal details.

Receiver
The receiver turns the electrical signal into what you hear. A sound is heard when the electric signal passes through an electromagnet, in turn pulling a diaphragm (made of steel) back and forth.

Microphone
The microphone's main job is to turn sound waves (from your voice) into electronic signals, which are then transmitted down the phone line.

Satellites
These days, instead of telephone exchanges, satellites that orbit around the earth bounce the electronic signals from one phone to another. Telephone masts do this as well.

The first commercial text message was sent in December 1992. Today the number of text messages sent and received everyday exceeds the total population of the entire planet.

The Satellites In Orbit_

On 4 October 1957 the world changed. The change wasn't necessarily obvious to everyone at the time but the implications of the successful launch and positioning of satellite **Sputnik** were immense. In effect it sounded the starting pistol for the **1960s Space Race** between USA and the Soviet Union, led to the first Moon landing and changed forever the way we communicate and the way we live. It also made the world much smaller.

Earth-orbiting satellite **Sputnik** was the size of a beach ball, about 58cm (23in) in diameter. Designed by a Soviet team headed by Sergei Korolev, it simply sent a beeping sound back to Earth for 23 days until its battery ran out. The 'beep' could be picked up all round the Earth as the shiny orb passed overhead. It carried on circling the Earth, each orbit taking 96 minutes and 12 seconds, until it burnt up on re-entering the atmosphere on 4 January 1958.

Since Sputnik first broke out of our atmosphere and flew above us, nearly 7,000 satellites (both **low Earth-orbiting** and **geostationary**) have been launched. Of these around 3,000 are orbiting the Earth, relaying data and monitoring the planet. The main activities of these are weather monitoring, communications, scientific research, navigation, Earth observation and military surveillance. Wherever you are now and whatever you are doing, someone, somewhere will be able to see you or hear you. Whether you're on your mobile, using your satnav in the car or just watching the big sports event on your television, you are not alone.

Something To Think About...

By the time Sputnik had come back down to Earth the Soviet Union had already launched its successor, Sputnik 2, on 7 November 1957. This was a bigger satellite and contained the first live animal to be sent out of our atmosphere. It was a dog, reportedly a laika breed, and its name was not known as it was a stray found on the streets of Moscow.

What satellites are used for

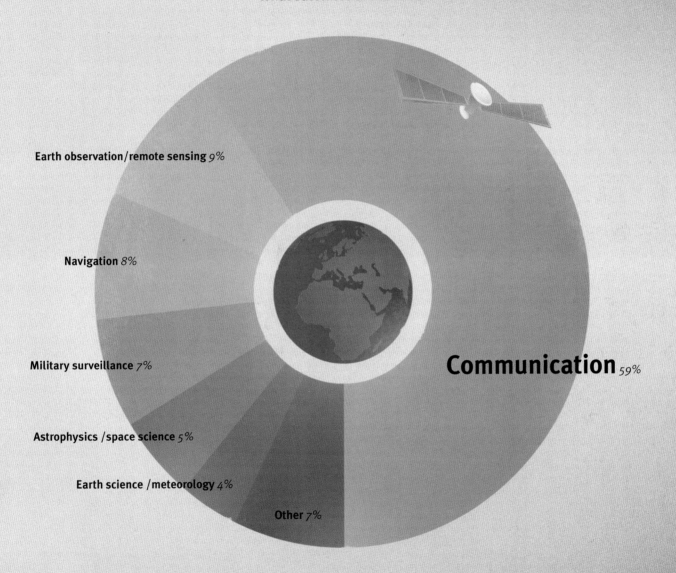

Earth observation/remote sensing *9%*

Navigation *8%*

Military surveillance *7%*

Astrophysics /space science *5%*

Earth science /meteorology *4%*

Other *7%*

Communication *59%*

[All figures from UCS Satellite Database, 2010.]

08.7 The Age Of Personal Computers_

In 1950 **computer scientist Alan Turing** predicted that by the turn of the millennium computers would have a billion bytes of memory – a preposterous statement at the time. In 2011, a 32gb smartphone – popular the world over – has approximately **32 billion bytes of memory**.

With the invention of the microchip almost anything became possible for the computer, and as their size has reduced, their speed has increased – there are almost no limits to what a computer can do. In 1974, the first 'real' Intel-made processor (a computer runs on microchips) the 8080, had 2,500 transistors. By 2004, the Intel 2 had 592 million!

MIPS (millions of instructions per second), the number of instructions that a computer can process in a second is, arguably, **the best indicator of a computer's speed** and shows how, since the invention of the first personal computer, computers have excelled in speed, function and memory.

Alan Turing's dream of **true artificial intelligence** has almost come to fruition and it will not be long before computers start inventing better versions of themselves. Science fiction and science fact are, it seems, coming closer together ...

Something To Think About ...

Gordon E. Moore was one of the founders of Intel – the largest semi-conductor chip-maker in the world. In 1965 he noted that the number of components used in a single computer chip doubled every year and saw no reason why this trend should not continue for at least ten years. In 1975 he altered this to be a doubling every *two years*. **Moore's Law** is both a statement and a target for hardware development in all sorts of areas, from the number of transistors on a chip, to the number of pixels per dollar you get in digital cameras.

The speed and development of the PC is shown
by this graph showing the MIPS (millions of
instructions per second) for many of the major
PC chips over the last 35 years.

Intel Core i7 Extreme *147,600*
(2010) – Where to next?

Intel Core 2 Extreme *59,455*
(2008) – 64-bit multi-core processing

IBM Xenon Triple Core *19,200*
(2005) – Used in the Xbox 360.

Intel Pentium 4 Extreme *9,726*
(2003) – 20,000 times faster than the 8080.

AMD Athlon *3,561*
(2000) – The first 1 GHz speed PC chip.

Intel Pentium III *1,354*
(1999) – High quality graphics.

Intel Pentium Pro *541*
(1996) – The beginning of the gaming PC.

Motorola 68060 *88*
(1994) – Higher end Macs and workstations.

Intel 486DX *54*
(1992) – Brought point-and-click to reality.

Motorola 68040 *44*
(1990)

Intel 386DX *11.4*
(1985)

Intel 286 *2.66*
(1982) – The MS-DOS PC chip.

Motorola 68000 *1*
(1979) – Apple Mac's processor.

Intel 8080 *0.5*
(1974) – The first 'real' PC chip.

The Growth Of The Internet_

The **World Wide Web** has been in existence since the end of 1991 thanks to **Sir Tim Berners-Lee**. The latest estimate of the number of web pages in existence is over 25 billion, although that has changed since you started reading this sentence. There are just under seven billion people on the planet so that is three pages each.

If each page was a piece of standard A4 paper and they were stacked in a pile, that pile would be 2,500km (1,553 miles) high – the same as driving from Glasgow to Rome.

Something To Think About ...

The first web page was:

http://www.w3.org/History/19921103-hypertext/hypertext/WWW/TheProject.html

It has no pictures and downloads in 1 nanosecond.

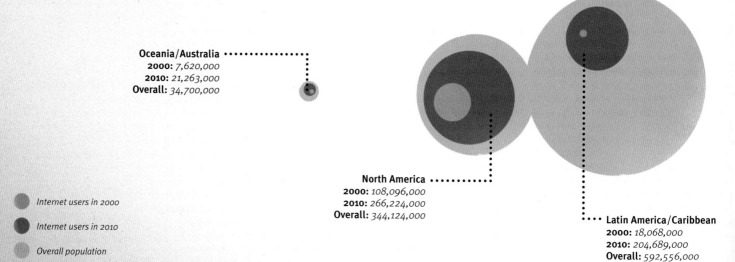

Oceania/Australia
2000: *7,620,000*
2010: *21,263,000*
Overall: *34,700,000*

North America
2000: *108,096,000*
2010: *266,224,000*
Overall: *344,124,000*

Latin America/Caribbean
2000: *18,068,000*
2010: *204,689,000*
Overall: *592,556,000*

Internet users in 2000

Internet users in 2010

Overall population

210, 000, 000, 000 e-mails are sent daily, an estimated 80% of which are spam.

While the number of people with access to the Internet is undoubtedly growing, this chart shows that there is still a large percentage of the population on each continent who don't have access.

Africa
2000: *4,514,400*
2010: *110,931,000*
Overall: *1,013,779,000*

Asia ....
2000: *114,304,000*
2010: *825,094,000*
Overall: *3,834,792,000*

Middle East
2000: *3,284,800*
2010: *63,240,000*
Overall: *212,336,000*

In 2010, there were on average 31 billion searches on Google every month.

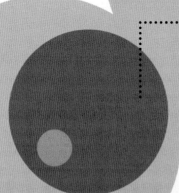

Europe
2000: *105,096,000*
2010: *475,069,000*
Overall: *813,319,000*

To reach a market audience of 50,000,000 people, it took the Internet just four years. By comparison, it took television 13 years and radio 38 years.

08.9 The World Of Social Networking_

If there was someone you went to school with but with whom you had lost touch, it is now possible, ridiculously easy in fact, to get in contact with them thanks to the phenomenon of Social Networking. With the Internet connecting everyone to potentially anyone, no one person is more than a couple of clicks away.

The concept of **Six Degrees of Separation**, whereby we are all linked to everyone else by no more than six links, has been proved beyond doubt with the rise of sites such as **Facebook**, **Twitter** and **Myspace**. Not only can you locate that long-lost school chum, it is now possible to feel that you are best friends with celebrities, politicians, or anyone on the planet.

www.classmates.com is considered to be the **first social networking site**. It was launched in 1995 and is still going strong. It has been overtaken by others and all social networking sites are swamped by Facebook.

Twitter is the latest major arrival and is slightly different from the others. It allows users to give their opinions and comments on anything but limits them to just 140 characters. Because followers spawn other followers, it has grown at an incredible rate.

Something To Think About...

Over 500 billion minutes are spent by users on Facebook each month. That's an average of 46 minutes a day per active user.

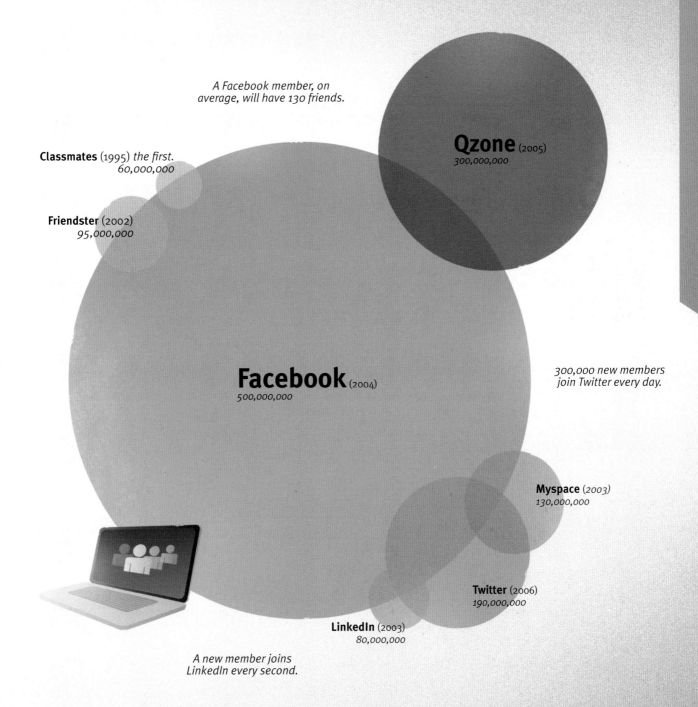

A Facebook member, on average, will have 130 friends.

Qzone (2005)
300,000,000

Classmates (1995) *the first.*
60,000,000

Friendster (2002)
95,000,000

Facebook (2004)
500,000,000

300,000 new members join Twitter every day.

Myspace (2003)
130,000,000

Twitter (2006)
190,000,000

LinkedIn (2003)
80,000,000

A new member joins LinkedIn every second.

Travelling Through Space_

In April 1950 a new comic strip hit the streets of the United Kingdom. Created and drawn by Frank Hampson, who had seen German rockets during the Second World War, it chronicled the adventures of Dan Dare, The Pilot of the Future. It was a fiction set in 1995 and the first voyage was to Venus in a desperate bid to find a new source of food for Earth as our resources ran out.

Hampson was ahead of the game. We have still not sent a man further than the Moon, but in principle he was right. It was the German expertise, shared between the Soviet Union and the USA, that was the driving force for **space exploration**.

The cost of space exploration is immense and so, since men first landed on the Moon, the costs have been kept down by sending unmanned craft. As well as the voyages to far-flung planets, the images gathered by the **Hubble Telescope** have added to our knowledge of what is out there. In some ways we have learnt more from Hubble than from the much further-travelled missions. The images it receives come from way beyond the distance that any ship has travelled.

As we enter the 21st Century, discussions are in process again about trying to send Man to another planet. As our finite resources begin to deplete, this may be because of actual need rather than just a thirst for knowledge.

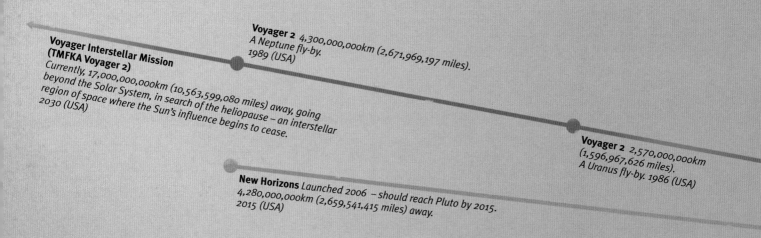

Voyager Interstellar Mission (TMFKA Voyager 2) Currently, 17,000,000,000km (10,563,599,080 miles) away, going beyond the Solar System, in search of the heliopause – an interstellar region of space where the Sun's influence begins to cease. 2030 (USA)

Voyager 2 4,300,000,000km (2,671,969,197 miles). A Neptune fly-by. 1989 (USA)

Voyager 2 2,570,000,000km (1,596,967,626 miles). A Uranus fly-by. 1986 (USA)

New Horizons Launched 2006 – should reach Pluto by 2015. 4,280,000,000km (2,659,541,415 miles) away. 2015 (USA)

Distances travelled of man-made crafts away from Earth.
[*Minimum distances used for orbital trajectories.]

Something To Think About ...

Only 12 men have walked on the surface of the Moon. The first to set foot on the surface was Neil Armstrong on 21 July 1969, the last was Eugene Cernan on 14 December 1972.

Pioneer 11 1,200,000,000km (745,665,817 miles). A Saturn fly-by. 1979 (USA)

Pioneer 10 893,000,000km (554,899,646 miles). A Jupiter fly-by. 1973 (USA)

Mars 2 55,000,000km (34,176,350 miles). Landed on Mars. 1972 (Soviet Union)

Mariner 10 77,000,000km (47,846,890 miles). A Mercury fly-by. 1974 (USA)

Venera 7 38,200,000km (23,737,029 miles). Landed on Venus. 1970 (Soviet Union)

Apollo 11 384,400km (238,861 miles). Manned spacecraft, landed on the Moon. 1969 (Neil Armstrong, Buzz Aldrin, USA)

Vostok 1 327km (203 miles). First human spaceflight. 1961 (Yuri Gagarin, Soviet Union)

Sputnik Earth-orbiting Satellite 945km (587 miles). 1957 (Soviet Union)

Hubble Space Telescope 550km (342 miles). Orbit. 1990 (USA)

International Space Station 350km (218 Miles). Orbit. 1998 (Various)

How Times Have Changed_

Life has changed beyond all recognition over the last 60 years and yet much has stayed the same. Over recent years, businesses and employers have seen a massive growth in the Internet, telecommunications and better travel making the working day simpler and easier for employees.

In the 1950s, in most developed countries, daily life was based very much around the immediate family and the home. It was easier to split the day into the three traditional segments of **sleep, work** and **leisure**. Due mainly to improvements in **medicine, nutrition** and **living standards** people are living, on average, ten years longer in developed nations. On the surface this should be a good thing, but it has problems.

With a **longer life expectancy** the average age of the population has risen and this generally means that, as a percentage of the population as a whole, there are more people not working. This puts an increased burden on the working population as they try to support the young and the retired. Whilst the number of hours at work in developed countries has remained almost constant – about eight hours a day – it is clear that time actually spent working has decreased due to social networking sites, the Internet and better global telecommunications.

Something To Think About...

In the developed world in the 1950s only 10% of households had a telephone. In the mid-1950s less than 30% of homes in the developed world had television sets. In 2010, over 85% have digital television sets.

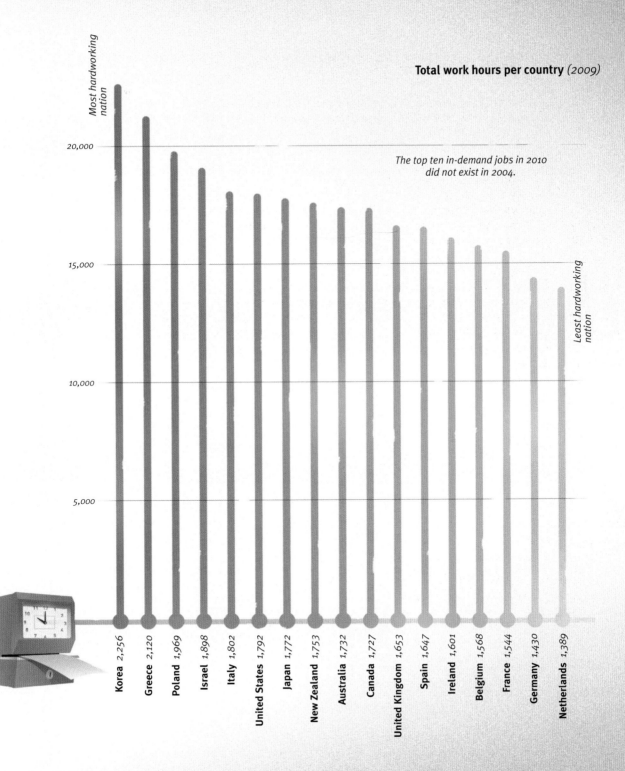

Total work hours per country (2009)

Most hardworking nation

The top ten in-demand jobs in 2010 did not exist in 2004.

Least hardworking nation

20,000

15,000

10,000

5,000

Korea 2,256
Greece 2,120
Poland 1,969
Israel 1,898
Italy 1,802
United States 1,792
Japan 1,772
New Zealand 1,753
Australia 1,732
Canada 1,727
United Kingdom 1,653
Spain 1,647
Ireland 1,601
Belgium 1,568
France 1,544
Germany 1,430
Netherlands 1,389

What Happens Next?

This book has looked at our planet, ourselves, and the way we live from the Big Bang right up until today. The one thing we cannot say with any certainty is what is going to happen tomorrow. Pessimists predict that **global warming** will eventually make life in most places impossible, that Earth's **natural resources** will run out and, like the dinosaurs, we will die out as a species, and eventually be replaced. The optimists look at what humans have achieved in our relatively short time on this globe and suggest that whatever happens we will find a way to survive. It may require that we all journey to another planet, or it may mean finding a safe **alternative to fossil fuels** and a way to feed an **ever growing population** without depleting the oxygen-giving rain forests.

We've all come a long way since that single, unifying moment 13.7 billion years ago that brought everything into being, but what we don't know is where we are on the journey. It is an overused cliché to say that if the life of this planet is 24 hours we are already at 23.59 and 59 seconds, but no one really knows.

As a species we may not know what will happen tomorrow but we have it in our power to shape what happens and it is this one significant fact that has made us different from the other living things that share our planet. We can make decisions that affect everything – but can we overcome our faults in order to do what is best?

The choice is yours but it could affect everyone's future.

Something To Think About ...

The world uses 85 million barrels of oil per day. A barrel is 158.9 litres (35 gallons), so that is 2 litres (2/5 gallon) per person, every single day.

Things of the future to look forward to – or not.

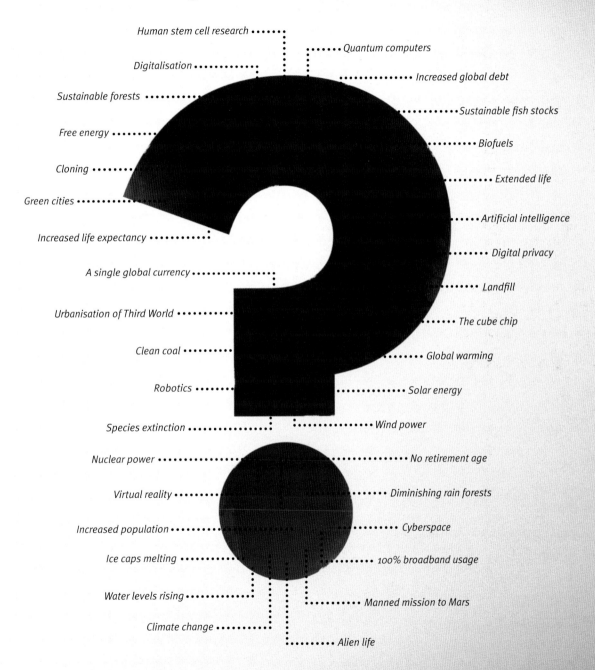

- Human stem cell research
- Quantum computers
- Digitalisation
- Increased global debt
- Sustainable forests
- Sustainable fish stocks
- Free energy
- Biofuels
- Cloning
- Extended life
- Green cities
- Artificial intelligence
- Increased life expectancy
- Digital privacy
- A single global currency
- Landfill
- Urbanisation of Third World
- The cube chip
- Clean coal
- Global warming
- Robotics
- Solar energy
- Species extinction
- Wind power
- Nuclear power
- No retirement age
- Virtual reality
- Diminishing rain forests
- Increased population
- Cyberspace
- Ice caps melting
- 100% broadband usage
- Water levels rising
- Manned mission to Mars
- Climate change
- Alien life

Index_

Index_ *cont.*

Daniel Tatarsky

Daniel was born in Liverpool. He now lives in London with his wife and his football boots. His interests are football, Subbuteo, cricket and baking. His first book was *Flick to Kick: An Illustrated History of Subbuteo*. He is the consultant editor for Orion Books' *Eagle* publishing programme and is the author of a biography of *Eagle*'s cover star Dan Dare.

Acknowledgements

I would like to thank Katie Cowan and Malcolm Croft for helping me turn a title into a fully-fledged book.

For the design of the book I am indebted to Zoe Anspach for getting the ball rolling in the right direction and Steve Russell for picking up the baton and running with it in marvellous fashion. Steve's contribution has spanned design, illustration and content and we could not have produced this book without him. Thanks also to Katie Hewett and Chris Stone for their eagle eyed editing and sage guidance.

Finally, I would like to dedicate this book to my dad Malcolm who left school at 13 but knew more than anyone I know and thus always beat my brothers and I at *Mastermind*, *A Question of Sport* and *Ask the Family*. And also my mum, Emmie, who genuinely believes that she knows Everything about Everything. Thanks fat legs.

Steve Russell

Steve was born and bred in Auckland, New Zealand. He has been based in London since 2006 where he works as a freelance designer and illustrator. He has designed books on just about every subject imaginable ... photography, tattoos, street art, cool caravans, war posters, ornithology, architecture, Maori language textbooks, a Japanese textbook and even a book about New Zealand hip hop.

You can see more of his work at www.aka-designaholic.com

Acknowledgements

I would like to thank everybody involved in this book, particularly Daniel Tatarsky, Katie Cowan and Malcolm Croft.

I would also like to thank Georgina Hewitt for hooking me up with Anova and also say a big thank you to all my friends and my flatmates for putting up with me while I spent endless hours working on this book.

This book is dedicated to my mother Margot Russell, because everything worthwhile I do will always be dedicated to her.

Oxygen

Electricity is electron... electrons move from atom to atom

Electricity travels at 300,000 kilometres per second. If a human being could travel that fast it could travel around the world eight times in the time it takes to switch on a light bulb.

Your brain generates between 10 and 25 watts of power – just enough to power a light bulb.

10,000

5,000

Current flow

Electron flow

Switch
Off/On

Battery/
Source

Light energy is converted into chemical energy by chlorophyll – a pigment that energises electrons using specific wavelengths of light. Chlorophyll is also what gives all plants their green colours.

A power source can be either direct current or alternating current. A battery is an example of the former and the charge is caused by a chemical reaction. A power station creates alternating current due to the movement of a magnet within a copper coil.

$C_6H_{12}O_6 + 6O_2$

Korea 2,256

Greece 2,120

Poland 2,469

Television
1925 – John Logie
Scotland

Telephone
1876 – Alexander Graham Bell
Canada

Powered flight
1903 – The Wright Brothers
USA

Toilet paper
14th Century China

Steam engine
1769 – James Watt
Scotland

Alphabet
2700 BC

АВГ
ФΨΞ

Automobile
1889 – Gottlieb Daimler
Germany

Electric w...
1906-ish

Printing press
1440 – Johannes Gutenberg
Germany

Electricity
1831 – Michael Faraday
England

Clock
1090 – Su Song
China

This graph shows the population change in major cities over the last 150 years